The Forgeries of
Jealousy

The Forgeries of Jealousy

Jealousy

Virginia Budd

PIATKUS

First published in Great Britain in 1990 by
Judy Piatkus (Publishers) Ltd of
5 Windmill Street, London W1

British Library Cataloguing in Publication Data
Budd, Virginia
  The Forgeries of jealousy.
  I. Title
  823'.914 [F]

  ISBN 0-7499-0019-9

Phototypeset in 11/12pt Compugraphic Times by
Action Typesetting Limited, Gloucester
Printed and bound in Great Britain by
Billing & Sons Ltd, Worcester

Titania These are the forgeries of jealousy:
And never, since the middle summer's spring,
Met we on hill, in dale, forest, or mead,
By paved fountain, or by rushy brook,
Or in the beached margent of the sea,
To dance our ringlets to the whistling wind,
But with thy brawls thou has disturbed our sport . . .

William Shakespeare *A Midsummer Night's Dream*

Chapter One

'I'm afraid the whole house needs rewiring, ma'am. These fuse boxes, I wouldn't care to say when they were put in — must be years back.'

'But it is safe? The thing is, my son and I aren't frightfully good with electrics and it would be too ghastly if the place caught fire. This old house would go up like a packet of crackers, and heaven alone knows where the nearest fire station is.'

'It's not that bad yet, ma'am, no need to worry. All the same, it best be done before the year's out. You can't trust this old wiring.'

Nerves twitching, Bet Brandon lit another cigarette, then discovered the tip was soggy; somehow or other in the general chaos, the packet seemed to have got soaked in tea. She didn't know what she was doing smoking anyway, she was supposed to have given it up months ago. She pulled herself together. 'The main thing is, it's all-right at the moment.'

'Let's say you won't be needing the fire engine yet awhile, ma'am, I wouldn't go further than that.' The man from the Electricity emerged from the cupboard in which he'd been crouching, and after carefully brushing the cobwebs out of his hair, replaced his uniform cap and picked up his bag of tools. He decided against any further words of caution, the lady looked harassed enough as it was. Instead he smiled, and with a flourish flicked the mains switch to 'On'. 'All-ready to cook your dinner now, ma'am, so I'll be on my way. And may I wish you and yours the very best of luck in your new home.'

'How ... how kind. Thank you so much for your help and — '

'They say they can't get that oak chest into the back bedroom, Mum, it won't go round the corner.' Diz Brandon, spectacles glinting, hair on end, a Roman candle of a boy whose enthusiasm was only increased by each fresh disaster, stood in the kitchen doorway. Just looking at him made his mother aware of her own exhaustion, and for a brief moment, as a solitary traveller in the desert might long for a cup of water, she longed to share his enthusiasm. 'All-right, I'm coming,' she said, vainly trying to remove the piece of damp cigarette paper adhering to her upper lip, 'but why on earth did they want to try and get it there in the first place? Any idiot could have seen it wouldn't go.'

'Do stop griping, Mum, I thought you said you wanted it up in that little room.'

'Of course I didn't. I meant the other chest, the one that was in Dad's study.'

'That your boy then, ma'am? Helping you out, is he?' The man from the Electricity shook with silent laughter, apparently convulsed at his own joke. He thrust a card into Bet's hand. 'Here's my card, ma'am, if you need me. I'll be on my way.' Her head was beginning to ache and she couldn't remember where she'd put down her cigarette. There came a distant shout from the removal men; to hell with the cigarette, the way she felt, she didn't care if the damn place did burn down.

Hours later, mother and son stood together in the front porch and watched the departing furniture van hit the gatepost. 'Silly buggers,' Diz said, pulling a piece of packing straw out of his hair, 'it must have been the tea you gave them.' Bet closed her eyes. She did wish he wouldn't make quite so many jokes. She decided to ignore this one. 'Well, all I can say is, I shall simply deduct whatever it costs to mend the gate from those wretched people's bill. Of all the moronic, inefficient outfits — and they weren't even cheap, either.'

'If you ask me, that old one was a bit past it, he had to sit down and have a quick rest after getting your bed upstairs and I didn't like the sound of his breathing, poor old devil.'

'In that case he shouldn't have been doing the job in the first place.'

'No choice probably, had to take what he could get. You can't chop and change jobs these days, Mum. He probably has a wife and ten kids to keep, and the DHSS aren't much help.'

'Look, darling, why don't you take Tib for a walk? He's been cooped up all day and it'll be dark soon. God knows where his lead is. If you can't find it you'd better use string, we don't want him running off.'

'OK, OK, I can take a hint! We might as well go down to the village, I'd like to have a nose round the place anyway.' Still bubbling, he hurried away. A moment later came the sound of hysterical barking, followed by pattering paws on carpetless stairs, then the slam of a distant door, then silence. Bet stayed where she was, hands in trouser pockets, looking up at the ossified remains of long dead files trapped in the cobwebs adhering to the porch ceiling. At her feet an angry black beetle, disturbed, crunched over the cracked tiles and scuttled to safety.

Perversely, now she was alone she realised that that was actually the last thing she wanted. Of course she would have to get used to being alone now, she had no option. What had Dr Ram said that last time she saw him? 'It is when the mourning time is over, Mrs Brandon, and ordinary life begins again, this is the time to watch. It is then that the psyche can play some strange tricks. I know this, Mrs Brandon, at first hand, and indeed it is true. My own very dear wife, when she passed on – it was hard, very hard. And it is harder still when friends say it is time to put away the grieving and stand upon one's own two feet . . . this is the testing time.' Bet shivered. Dear, wise Dr Ram, if only he were here now.

Suddenly a swallow swooped down out of nowhere, making her jump, then just as suddenly vanished. Hadn't the swallows gone yet, it must be time, surely? She stepped out of the porch on to the churned-up gravel and squinted up at the sky. What a perfect day, and this was the first time she'd noticed it. Sun shone through high, flying white clouds, the sky was a brilliant blue, there was a hint of gold and brown in the trees. Rooks cawed evocatively from their colony in the cedar tree that reared massively out of the unkempt lawn; from somewhere in the woods across the fields behind it came the raucous cry of a cock pheasant. Bet turned her face to the sun, blinking in its warmth, and unexpectedly felt a twinge of excitement almost childlike in its intensity. When on earth had she last felt like that? Not for years and years, not since she and Miles were married. She smiled, seeing herself from outside, as one did as a child: a heroine in a romance, winning a beauty competition or the Latin prize at school, marrying a duke, saving someone from drowning. What was the name of that book Dad used to read to them? *Maddy and the Haunted Rectory.* How she'd longed to be Maddy!

'The psyche can play some strange tricks ...' And what on earth, she wondered, as she pulled off the scarf she'd worn round her head all day and let the warm air blow through her hair, had Dr Ram meant by that? She stood there for another minute, thinking about it, then with a shrug (she would no doubt find out soon enough if there was anything to find out) turned back into the house, shutting the front door firmly behind her. What she needed now was a drink, and if it was only half-past five, too bad!

Plonked down at the table in the big, old-fashioned kitchen, surrounded by half-empty packing cases and unfinished cups of tea, the only sounds the humming of the fridge and the chattering of a magpie outside in the yard, she reached for the half-bottle of gin she'd had the wit to bring with them from London and poured herself a generous measure. There was nothing but tap water to top it up with, so that the first sip or two tasted like medicine, but after that she forgot the taste and simply let the alcohol run through her; dangerous, deadening, blurring the edges of life. One could get used to this! She took another sip and wondered what Miles would say if he could see her.

Perhaps he could; perhaps against all odds he might be able to. But he wouldn't mind, he'd know she had good reason for doing it. That was how Miles was, sensible, tolerant, kind. Dear Miles! She dug her nails into the palms of her hands so hard it hurt. Dr Ram had suggested she try this, and to her surprise it worked — the sharp, physical pain serving, just for the time being, to blot out the agony of loss. Now, as the pain receded, she felt safe to let her mind wander back over the events of the past year. Perhaps, after all, they had been

4

lucky. It had all happened so quickly. A year ago they had had absolutely no inkling of what was about to happen.

She and Miles had just returned from holiday, a busy winter ahead of them; Nell was married and living in Fulham, Diz was studying for next summer's GCSEs. There was a routine visit to the doctor – Miles's tummy was playing up; holiday food, they'd thought, too much oil. An X-ray and . . . there it was. Three months or possibly less, the hospital had said. In fact it was only six weeks.

They'd said goodbye in New End Hospital, Hampstead, its antiseptic tower block and whizzing lifts more like an airport than a hospital. 'I'm sorry, my duck,' Miles said, 'I don't seem able to crack this one. I know you're supposed to be able to reverse cancer, but it seems beyond me; perhaps I didn't have enough time.' He was quiet for a minute, reserving his strength. 'I suppose, as an experience, there's an outside chance it might be an interesting one – death, I mean. It's you . . .' He paused again. 'Please be all-right. Financially you'll be OK – just about. The kids will survive, Nell has Bernard, and Diz will work something out. But you . . .'

'I'll be all-right,' she had said. 'You mustn't worry about me.' But then of course she hadn't known, couldn't even have imagined, what life without him would be like.

After that she remembered standing outside the hospital, looking down towards South End Green at the winter trees stark above the scurrying traffic, and thinking that this was going to be far worse than anything that had ever happened to her before.

Of the weeks immediately following Miles' death she recalled very little. Had she been doped? The funeral was a blur. A lot of that time she'd felt angry, she did know that. She supposed she must have behaved fairly well – long training as the wife of a liberal-minded civil servant would have taken care of that – but the anger had been there all right, in fact still was. Another thing she remembered was overhearing her sister, Pol, talking to a friend on the phone – 'My dear, Bet's coping marvellously, but of course one knew she would' – and for some reason feeling quite murderous.

But almost the worst thing had been Tib. Miles was a dog

5

man – in the main, he once confessed, preferring dogs to people – and Tib was an integral part of the household. Every weekday evening he would position himself from six o'clock onwards at Miles's study window, waiting to be the first to spot his master's tall, weary figure, briefcase under arm, climbing the steep, winding hill that led from Hampstead tube station to their house. At the sound of Miles's key in the lock he would rush into the hall, paws scrabbling wildly on the parquet floor, to greet him as he opened the front door ... After Miles's death Tib became quite simply inconsolable. Diz did his best; had him to sleep on his bed, took him for long walks on Hampstead Heath, tried to make him play with his ball, but all to no avail. For weeks he barely ate, never relaxed, listened endlessly for the click of a key in the lock, the sound of a voice: 'Hullo Tibby, you lazy sod, and what have you been up to today.'

When was it she'd first realised she no longer wanted to stay on in Thorn Lane? She and Miles had bought no. 10 Thorn Lane, Hampstead, soon after their marriage; it was the only home Nell and Diz had ever known, and naturally enough everyone assumed she would go on living there – she did herself. It was Mr Tyler's visit that had triggered things off. He'd come to clear a blocked drain. 'You'll be needing that guttering renewed before next winter, Mrs Brandon,' he said as they stood together in the back garden peering up at the roof, and she'd thought suddenly. But I won't be here next winter, I simply could not bear to be.

At first she told no one of her growing feeling against the house – guilt, perhaps. Why she should have felt guilty she wasn't sure, but she had. Despite the guilt, though, the feeling wouldn't go away, and as the daffodils began to flower once again in the smart little gardens behind the smart little houses of Thorn Lane, so her longing to leave the place grew. She found herself beginning to hate the Hampstead she had loved: the people, the traffic, the trendy boutiques and bijou restaurants; and, at last, the house itself.

When she finally got round to broaching the subject of a possible move to Diz, his reaction came as something of an anti-climax. 'Why not?' he said listlessly. 'If it's me you're worrying about, don't. Once I've done GCSEs this summer,

6

I can easily do my A-levels somewhere else − unless, that is, you were planning to go away somewhere on your own?'

'Of course I wasn't planning to go somewhere on my own!' she'd shouted. Ever since Miles' death she seemed to feel she could only get through to people by shouting. 'Don't over-react, Bet,' Pol said, 'we're not all deaf. I know you've been through a lot, but all the same . . . ' 'That's all right then,' Diz had said, and gone on doling out Pedigree Chum for Tib's dinner.

Two days later Nell came to tea and produced her plan.

Nell and Bernie had been married a year by then. They'd met originally at an office party given one Christmas by the monster insurance group for which they both worked. Initially, neither Bet nor Miles had greatly taken to Bernie Sparsworth. Indeed, Miles remained lukewarm until the end, and had never got beyond addressing his son-in-law formally as Bernard. Bernie was a small, dark, fashion-conscious young man with a drooping Edwardian moustache, who wore what he called three-piece suits in the very latest style, and went in for jogging. He was one of the very few people Bet knew who, against all odds, continued to maintain the nineteenth-century view of the inevitable progression of the human race; citing, with an optimism touching in its simplicity, anything from the microchip to the latest fast food revolution to prove his point. Miles always claimed that Bernie secretly believed real history had only begun at his, Bernie's, birth in 1953. Nevertheless, Nell and Bernie did seem ideally suited − even Miles admitted it. Nell and her father were never close, indeed Nell had always been a little frightened of him. He would occasionally make a sarcastic remark, cutting across her innocuous chatter, and she would flush and her voice take on a shrill note, the aggressive pose hiding the very real hurt. She had been upset by her father's death, but not in the same way as Diz.

It was a warm day in late May, with the stink of petrol and exhaust fumes rising miasma-like above Hampstead, and the two of them were sitting in the back garden having tea, when Nell let loose her bombshell. The words came out in a rush, as though prepared beforehand, and at the end she had looked at her mother as one expecting, at the very least, a blow on the

7

head for having the audacity to propose such a plan.

It had resulted initially, it appeared, from the fact that Bernie was to be transferred to the insurance group's head office at Stourwick in Suffolk – a step up the promotion ladder that could not possibly be refused. In any case they both wanted to move out of London, the flat in Fulham being no place to bring up a family. To this end they had begun house-hunting in Suffolk at weekends. However, despite the fact that the group gave substantial help over mortgages, every property they liked proved to be way above their price range – 'You know Bernie, Mum, he's such a perfectionist' – and after several weeks of fruitless searching they'd begun to get pretty fed up. Then they'd gone out for a meal one evening with Aunt Pol and Uncle Pete – 'That new place in the Kings Road, the one with lots of salads and all those statues' – and the idea had suddenly come to them. Aunt Pol had just said how she longed to have a little place in the country for weekends, and Suffolk seemed as good a county as any to start looking, when Uncle Pete said out of the blue, How about buying a house together and cutting it in half? She and Bernie could live in one half and he and Aunt Pol could use the other half as their weekend base. The advantages of this plan, as Uncle Pete saw it, were twofold: first, they could jointly afford a much better place, and second, the Sparsworths could keep a watching brief on his and Aunt Pol's part of the house when they were away during the week.

'Good old Pete, always one eye on the main chance,' Bet hadn't been able to resist interrupting at this point. Nell looked at her reproachfully. 'Mum, please!'

Well, of course the next thing had been. What about Diz and Mum left all on their own in Hampstead? And quick as a flash someone said – Nell couldn't now remember who – Why can't they come too, then we could buy an even bigger and better house? 'You see, Mum, Diz had already told us you were fed up with Thorn Lane and didn't want to stay on here. And if you came too we could get something really good with a big garden. You know how you love gardening and are always complaining you can't do it properly in London. Bern's brilliant at DIY and, well, we just thought . . .'

'I take it,' Bet said, 'you've already discussed all this with Diz?'

'Well, yes, as a matter of fact we have. He thought it a great idea, he — '

'Naturally, I'm the last to be told.'

'Please, Mum, don't make things difficult, we only meant it for the best. It seemed such a great idea, all of us together in a new place . . .' Nell's voice petered out and she took a gulp of tea. Silence fell between them while they listened to the distant rumble of traffic on Haverstock Hill, bisected now and again by the moan of a police siren or the roar of a jet. In truth Bet was not only intrigued, but astonished by the whole, bold scheme; she hadn't thought these particular members of her family capable of producing an idea of such originality. She felt a twinge of excitement, a stirring of interest; it was like tentatively putting one's foot to the ground after a long illness. Still, one shouldn't sound too enthusiastic at first.

'Well,' she had said at last, 'it's certainly an original idea and it has distinct possibilities, but I'm not sure about . . .'

And that was how it began.

Of course there were snags, not the least of them being Pol and Pete. Bet's sister, Polly Redford, was three years her junior. She and Pete, married in 1962, had never produced any children. They lived, more or less harmoniously, in a smart little house in Chelsea, had a new car every two years, and entertained their friends to cosy dinner parties where the drink flowed freely, everyone made token passes at everyone else's wife and of course nobody minded. The Redfords had for some years talked of buying a cottage in the country, a weekend retreat in which to unwind in some arcane village setting, but for one reason or another the plan had never come to fruition — until now.

On thinking things over after Nell had gone, Bet could see that from her sister's point of view, house-sharing would have a great many advantages; a built-in housekeeper for a start, a gardener, too, for that matter. But she was forced to admit that she herself would also benefit from such a scheme. Sharing a house with Pol after so many years would certainly be a challenge, might even turn out to be a test of endurance — but it could hardly be worse, she felt, than her present situation.

The relationship between Bet and her sister had always been a complex one. Ever since childhood, for reasons unclear to Bet, she had felt guilty about Pol — and, surprisingly, the guilt had continued even after Pol married and became considerably better off than Miles and herself. Pol did little to dispel her guilt, in fact made it worse by somehow always managing to give the impression that, although she herself was having a simply marvellous time, somewhere just round the corner Bet was having an even better one. That Bet had two children and Pol none, oddly enough had never been an issue. Indeed, Pol was closer to Nell than Bet was; they had always got on, ever since Nell, as a toddler, had fancifully likened her aunt to 'a beautiful fairy on a Christmas tree'.

Bet's feelings about her brother-in-law were more straight forward. Pete was all-right really. Under his pose of City gent/Tory backwoodsman, he was a simple, kindly soul. After the war, his father, who had been a minor civil servant, went into partnership with a man he met in a pub and made a fortune out of scrap metal overnight. Pete had been sent to a minor public school which he hated — or so, in a drunken moment, he had once admitted to Bet — but always publicly referred to his years there as the best of his life — and if anyone chose to believe the school was Eton, that was their affair. After doing his National Service as a corporal in REME — again, if anyone chose to believe he'd been a second lieutenant in the Guards he wouldn't disillusion them — he went into a stock-broking office in the City, where he discovered to his considerable surprise that he was absolutely brilliant at making money. Over the years he had kept his rather florid good looks, and apart from a slight thinning of his blonde hair, a tendency to breathlessness and a budding double chin, he still looked pretty much as he had when Pol married him.

The snag about Pete, from Bet's point of view was that in the last few years he'd taken to falling in love with young and unlikely girls, and using Bet as an embarrassed confidante. Since Miles' death she had heard little of his activities on this front, but found it hard to believe they had ceased. Pol, cocooned as she was in her own self-esteem, appeared never to have doubted Pete's devotion, and Bet passionately hoped this state of affairs would continue, for all their sakes. Miles had always tended to treat Pete as something of a joke figure, often repeating, in a take-off of Pete's plummy Old Etonian accent, his brother-in-law's latest statement on world affairs. Bet and Diz always fell about laughing, and it was only afterwards, when Nell put on her prim face — not daring to voice her disapproval in front of her father — that Bet would experience a twinge or two of guilt. For the truth was that she loved Pete, and his kindness and understanding of her pain following Miles's death had been a revelation.

Despite the doubts and anxieties, however, a decision was made at last. The house in Thorn Lane was put on the market and house-hunting in Suffolk began in earnest. At first they'd been flooded with particulars of perfectly splendid-looking properties, every last one turning out to have a fatal flaw not mentioned by the estate agents. A buyer was found for Thorn Lane, ready and anxious to exchange contracts — an up-and-coming actor and his live-in girlfriend — but still they'd found nothing. Then at last, when hope was almost gone, one pouring wet Sunday afternoon at the end of July, with Pete driving, Diz map-reading, Bet and Tib penned up in the back, they found it.

The Old Rectory, Hopton, 'in need of some modernisation and repair', was the last house on the day's list, the agent's particulars so bald that they'd nearly left them behind, feeling a visit would simply turn out to be a waste of time. However, the house did have the right number of bedrooms, and it was only three o'clock — they might as well just take a quick look.

At first sight Hopton village was pretty uninspiring, especially in the rain. There was the usual fuzz of 1950s council houses, there were two newly-built council estates, and there was a main street which, as in many Suffolk villages, straggled on for nearly three-quarters of a mile. Pete drove slowly past a row of cottages, the rain thudding on the car roof, and stopped beside a village ancient with a sack draped round his shoulders. The ancient pointed a quavering finger. 'Over bridge and bear round to the right, can't miss ut, gate's just past church.' And there it had been, a Jane Austen

11

rectory, simple, sensible and beautiful, with a cedar tree, a jumble of stables and a real walled vegetable garden. 'Oh God,' she'd whispered into Tib's ear, 'we've found it,' and prayed the others would think so too. Tib shot out of the car and disappeared, Diz put on his enigmatic face – so like Miles – which meant that underneath he was very excited indeed, and Pete, after a long look round, said: 'It needs a lot doing to it, of course, but it does have possibilities. If we can bring the price down a bit ... get a grant ...'

Deeds were signed, builder's estimates discarded. After much wrangling and discussion, crucial decisions were made about who should have which part of the house, and whether to divide it into two or three; in the end they plumped for two, with Bet, Diz and the Sparsworths living more or less together, though of course they all had their own rooms. It all took a long time, harsh words were spoken and tempers lost, but somehow or other, as the leaves were beginning to turn on the Heath, Bet, Diz and Tib had left no. 10 Thorn Lane, Hampstead, for ever, and here they were, the vanguard of their little army, two intrepid explorers of a new world ...

Bet shivered. She felt cold and slightly sick; she should have eaten, not drunk. She supposed she'd better get some sort of meal together. Oven-ready chips and beefburgers, their last purchase from the shop round the corner in Kingsland Avenue. 'Goodbye, dear Mrs Brandon,' Mr Gopal had said, squeezing her hand rather too tightly for comfort, 'we will be missing you a great deal here,' and she almost ran out of the shop for fear he should see her cry. She hadn't even stopped to check her change, sometimes necessary with Mr Gopal, but one never minded having to, he was always so sympathetic. She shivered again. Surely it shouldn't be so cold in here on such a lovely day? Damp, of course. No doubt endemic – all rectories were damp. Oh God, they'd never get the place right! The future loomed unbearably – what little money she had wasted on incompetent damp-proof experts and ex-orbitant heating bills.

It was all the miserable Bernie's fault for refusing Pete's offer. 'We'll start as we mean to go on, Pete, thanks all the same,' he'd said primly – presumably using 'we' in the regal sense, for Bet herself had no such inhibitions – when Pete

12

offered to lend them the money for central heating. 'It's your decision, old boy, of course,' Pete responded, 'but one would have thought it better to have the whole house done in one go rather then fiddle around separately. Cheaper, too, in the long run.' But Bernie, to Bet's annoyance − and even Nell had looked a bit wistful − merely shook his head. 'I'm thinking in terms of solid fuel, actually, Pete,' he said, looking keenly round the table at the circle of unresponsive faces, 'there's no doubt SF is the fuel of the future, and with some of these new systems, only half the price of gas. Anyway, I'd like to shop around a bit before I come to any decision. There's a guy in our Life department who's quite an expert.'

At this point Pol had looked at Bet, obviously expecting her to speak up, say that of course they would accept Pete's offer, it would be absurd not to. But she hadn't spoken up, she'd just sat there and sulked, preferring to remain a member of the rank and file and let Bernie take responsibility for organising the heating − or anything else for that matter − in their part of the house. Was that what twenty-eight years of marriage did to you? Made you lose the power of positive decision-making? Made you work on the principle that if there was a man in the vicinity, it might be easier − even better − if he took charge? Pretty feeble, really, when you thought about it, but there it was. And Bernie, the self-opinionated young ass, had his way; the net result being that while the Redfords would bask in a steady temperature of seventy-five degrees this winter, the rest of them, compelled to make do with an as yet untried and extremely ancient Rayburn and a few assorted electric fires, would freeze.

Central heating, or the lack of it, wasn't the only dissimilarity between the two sections of Hopton Rectory either. Pete and Pol's half − the south wing, consisting of the rector's old study, a butler's pantry and the back stairs leading to two bedrooms and an antediluvian bathroom − had already undergone gigantic changes, and although still far from complete, it was well on its way to becoming the luxury pad Pol claimed was absolutely essential to country living. Not really in Bet's style, of course, which was one consolation, but nevertheless pretty impressive. In contrast, to date, the Brandon/Sparsworth end of the house had been left virtually untouched. Apart from some necessary adjustments to the plumbing, a few new tiles on the roof and the sanding of the floor in Bet's sitting-room — she wasn't going to have Miles's Persian rugs slumming it on six layers of khaki linoleum — nothing had been done. Bernie was the expert on DIY, let him get on with it. All she was interested in was the garden anyway.

The phone rang as she was scrabbling through one of the many plastic shopping bags they'd brought with them, vainly looking for the beefburgers. It was the first time the phone had rung since they arrived; its bell sounded wheezy and full of dust.

'Hullo?'

'Oh, hullo. Am I speaking to the rector's wife? I'm chairman of the Little Podlington Unmarried Mothers' Association — '

'I'm sorry, Pete, but I'm not in the mood for jokes. It's been the most ghastly day. Say what you have to say and then get off the line, I'm in the middle of cooking the first meal Diz and I've had in twenty-four hours.'

'Don't be like that, ducky, I was only ringing to see how you're getting on ...'

The oven-ready chips were in the oven and she was upstairs making up the beds, when Diz and Tib arrived back, accompanied, inexplicably, by a cross-looking young man in a raspberry-coloured vest and jeans. *Now* what? Bet pushed up the window and stuck her head out. 'Hullo?'

'Is this your dog?'

'Of course it is. Who — ?'

'You're lucky I haven't called the police, then. It's vicious. It chased our cat up a tree, and when my wife tried to stop it, it went for her. You should keep the animal under proper control, you know, instead of letting it run wild all over our estate.'

'He's talking utter rubbish, Mum. Tib wasn't out of control at all, and if people can't tell the difference between a friendly greeting and a vicious attack, all I can say is they should get themselves a doctor. I just — '

'Diz!' It came out in a sort of strangled shriek, and if

14

nothing else, served to stop the two young men in their tracks. Having gained the advantage she'd better make use of it – was this positive decision-making? 'I don't wish to hear any more, Desmond. Take Tib round to the kitchen at once and shut him in. You can give him his dinner, I've unpacked his stuff. At once, d'you hear. I don't want any argument.'

'Christ, Mum!' Diz, red in the face, his body rigid with outrage, stood blinking up at her, the evening sun shining on his spectacles. She felt a twinge of love. 'Surely you've at least got the decency to listen to my side?' he said. 'That oaf threw a stone at Tib. It could have cut him quite badly, he – '

'Scram!' Why on earth had she used such a very outdated expression? But to her surprise it worked. After a moment's shocked, reproachful silence, her son, with a grossly exaggerated shrug of the shoulders, turned on his heel and crunched heavily away across the gravel, dragging Tib behind him. She'd won!

'I'm so sorry, Mr . . . ?'

'Bone, if you must know, but – '

'Mr Bone. I'll be down in a second. I was making up the beds, you see we've only just moved in . . .'

A rapid glance in the mirror, a smear of lipstick and a squirt of that expensive perfume Pete had given her last Christmas. What was she trying to do, flaunt her sexuality (always supposing she still had any) in order to get this ghastly young man to climb down? She opened the front door. 'Do please come in, Mr Bone. I'm so sorry about all this. Could I possibly offer you a drink? I'm sure we have some somewhere.'

Half an hour later, dog forgotten, slightly pink about the gills and smiling gently to himself, Brian Bone returned to Buttercup Close. What was a bird like that doing all on her own in a house like that with a son like him? Getting on a bit, but so was Liz Taylor, and he sometimes dreamed about Liz Taylor. Would he dream about Mrs Brandon? Well he wouldn't mind! What with Moira expecting, and wanting him to kip in the spare room . . .

He slid through the front door of no. 8, his trainers making no noise on the brown-and-orange-patterned brush-nylon carpeting. 'Bri, where have you been all this time? Mum says

15

we ought to call the police and lay charges. These people shouldn't be allowed to get away with it — that boy!'

Brian groaned. He'd hoped she wouldn't hear him come in. He put on his soothing voice — used more and more frequently as the weeks of Moira's pregnancy dragged by. 'Calm down, pet. It's all turned out to be a bit of a storm in a teacup. Mrs Brandon's a widow, on her own, like, got a lot to cope with. She was quite upset. And you didn't have to go and ring your mum.'

But there was no reply. Moira Bone was on her way to the bathroom. She was going to be sick again.

Chapter Two

'Mrs Redford on the line, Pete. Shall I put her through?'
Wiggins Apthorp encouraged informality in their employees,
Mr Bellman, the senior partner, taking the view that despite
certain obvious dangers, such a policy paid off in the long
run.

Pete groaned. Christmas had come and gone, but the
Redfords' wing of Hopton Rectory remained uninhabitable.
They'd spent the holiday staying with friends in the Bahamas
and had just returned, tanned and overfed, to the bleak reality
of a London January. 'I suppose you'd better. What on earth
can she . . . ? Oh hullo, darling, anything wrong?'

'Of course there's something wrong, I wouldn't be ringing
you if there wasn't. I've just had the builders on the phone.
They say they can't be finished by next week. Some nonsense
about having to wait for something to dry before they can do
anything else. Just an excuse for skiving, of course, you know
what these people are.'

Pete sipped a mouthful of cold coffee; it tasted of TCP.
What on earth did Fiona do to get it like that? 'Well, we'll just
have to postpone the move, that's all, there's not a lot else we
can do. Does Cameron say when they think they will be out?
Why not have a word with Bet?'

'I've spoken to Bet already. I rang her to ask about finding
a daily.'

'What did she say about Cameron?'

'Nothing really, you know Bet. Just said the place was still
in a frightful mess and Mr Cameron was a nice man and doing
his best. Honestly, I simply don't know how Bet's going to

cope in the real world; she's had Miles to wet-nurse her for so long ...'

Pete's eyes wandered longingly in the direction of his *Financial Times*. He twitched it towards him. Unfortunately he twitched too hard and managed to upset his still half-filled cup of coffee. A stream of khaki-coloured liquid trickled gently over the newspaper and down on to the expensive rug underneath his desk. 'Bloody hell!'

'Pete, are you listening?'

'Of course I am, it's just I've upset my coffee. I'll have to get Fiona to clear it up before it soaks in.' Pol snorted. 'Do you ever do any work? I haven't even had time yet for a slice of toast, let alone mid-morning coffee.'

'Look, ducky, I'll ring the Rectory this afternoon, have a word with Bet — and Cameron, if I can get hold of him — but quite frankly I don't see the world falling apart because we can't move down there for another week or two. Now I really must go, old girl, there's a call from New York on the other line.' He quickly replaced the receiver before she could say anything else. 'Fiona, love, can you come in? I'm afraid there's been a disaster with your coffee ...'

That afternoon, pleasantly relaxed after a heavy lunch, Pete put a call through to the Rectory. Would Bet be in one of her moods? He loved talking to Bet, she terrified him and excited him at the same time; like a nervous thoroughbred horse, you never knew what she would do next, kick out at you or smile that lovely smile of hers. Wasted on old Miles really. All those years stuck in Hampstead, reading the *Guardian,* canvassing for the Labour party and organising jumble sales for War on Want. He wondered what she would do now, let loose on the world after so long. She'd loved Miles Brandon totally, he'd always known that. But occasionally, just very occasionally, he'd glimpsed another quality in her; a kind of harsh sexuality quite out of keeping with her role of liberal-minded Hampstead housewife and mother.

'Hullo, hullo! How's my favourite sister-in-law? I gather there's been a spot of bother with our esteemed friend Cameron?'

'Look, Pete, before you go any further I should just like to say that I've quite enough to do down here without having to

18

spend half my time relaying totally unnecessary messages to your wretched builders. I'm not surprised they're behind, Mr Cameron says Pol changed her mind six times over the bathroom wallpaper and then went back to the first one they'd tried. He was practically in tears, he . . .'

Pete closed his eyes. Bet always looked so delicious when she was cross. He tried to imagine her standing there by the phone, one slim, brown hand gripping the receiver, her hair bouncing about on her shoulders — the colour of sweet dark sherry, he'd once poetically described it, and even after all these years it was still like that except for one or two interesting streaks of grey at the temples. Her green eyes would be all stormy and tragic-looking, and . . . 'Pete, are you still there or has some idiot cut us off?'

'I'm still here, ducky.'

'Answer my question, then. Do you or do you not know that Pol is now insisting on having a daily? Not only that, but expecting me to scour the neighbourhood for one.'

'Actually, ducky, I think she only wants one twice a week — someone to get things ready before we come down on a Friday and clear up afterwards on a Monday. The place will probably be a bit of a shambles; you see, the old girl means to do quite a lot of entertaining.'

'It's a pity she couldn't have told me that in the first place. Now I'll have to rewrite the notice I was going to put in the Post Office.'

'What a bore for you, ducky, Pol should have made it clearer.' Did he sound sympathetic enough? 'Look Bet, you've been an absolute brick these last weeks, you really have. The last thing I want to do is add to your worries, it's just . . . well, you know Pol.'

'I do indeed.' There was silence. Would she hang up on him? 'Are you still there, ducky?'

'Of course I'm still here. I just don't have anything else to say. Mr Cameron, as far as I can tell, is doing wonders; the place looks like something out of *Ideal Home* and if Pol would only stop messing him about he would have finished weeks ago.'

'Well, that is splendid news, really splendid. Old Felix's cousin, Monty Cornwall, put us on to Cameron, you know.

19

He has a place in Suffolk — Monty Cornwall, I mean, not Cameron. Frightfully good chap, Felix says, brother in the Rifle Brigade. We'll have him over and you must meet. Of course he knows everyone in the county, the Cornwalls have been there since the flood.'

'Aren't you afraid I might let the side down? Currently the only person I've met, apart from the vicar, is a young plumber from one of the housing estates. He came to complain about Tib. Diz says he's fallen for me.'

'We'll soon change all that.' Pete tried not to feel disturbed by this news. Hobnobbing with plumbers from the local housing estate, not quite his and Pol's line of country! He suddenly realised the time. He'd promised to be home early, Pol was giving one of her dinner parties. 'Must go now, ducky. And as I've said, don't worry about a thing. I'm sure old Monty Cornwall's wife will be able to rustle up a daily if the worst comes to the worst.'

'To hell with old Monty Cornwall and his wife!'

Pete smiled. He loved Bet when she said things like that.

Back at no. 6 Parsley Street, Pol greeted him tearfully. 'The Cardews can't come, she's got flu. He only rang five minutes ago so there's no time to get hold of anyone else. It really is the limit. How can people be so inconsiderate. And what, may one ask, does one do with all this food?'

Pete's heart sank.

'All I said was, I'm a little tired of being used by Aunt Pol as some sort of go-between.'

'I realize that, Mum, but you must admit that if you and Aunt Pol spend your time sniping at each other over the phone before she's even moved in, it doesn't augur too well for the future. Know what I mean?'

'Please don't use that expression, Diz. If I don't understand what you mean, I'll say so.' Bet peered gloomily at the potato she was scrubbing. Was she becoming a nag? Probably; old Ma in the kitchen amongst the pots, shrieking instructions that no one listened to, every other sentence an expostulation, if not an expostulation a gripe. All the same, it wasn't fair, was it, Pol spending her Christmas lying on a beach doing damn-all while she slaved away here freezing to death.

'The trouble with you, Mum,' Diz nibbled at a raw carrot, 'is that you always have to go to such extremes. All you needed to do was to say to Aunt Pol quite calmly and quietly that you did just happen to – '

'Look, Diz, when I want your advice on how to deal with my sister, I'll ask for it. What are you doing down here anyway? Shouldn't you be working?'

'The learning factory doesn't encourage work at home. Rightly or wrongly, they feel the home environment is not conducive to study, and looking round here, who am I to argue? Besides, I've promised to help Bern paint their sitting-room this evening. We're getting in some cans of beer and making a night of it.'

'Well, see you don't make too much of a night of it, that's all. And ask Bernie not to wash his brushes in my sink this time, he can use the one in the old pantry.'

They had been at the Rectory nearly four months now, and the Sparsworths nearly three. It was early days yet, but now that Nell had got herself a job in Stourwick with a firm of solicitors and was consequently out of the house all day, things were settling down quite well. Before this happened, Bet had to admit that life had not always been easy. Odd that with all her worrying about how she and Pol would get on living in the same house, it had never crossed her mind to worry about how she and Nell would get on. Had Nell ever wondered about how she would get on with Bet? She'd never said anything – but then she wouldn't, would she? What both of them had forgotten, of course, in the excitement of moving and making a start in a new place, was that Nell had been undisputed queen of her own domestic domain for the past eighteen months; and although her mother had been queen of *hers* for the past twenty-eight years Nell naturally had no intention whatsoever of relinquishing any of her newly acquired power.

Matters hadn't been helped by the fact that Nell was such a hopeless cook. She tried, God knows she tried, following the instructions on each new recipe with the fanaticism of a scientist working on the blueprint of a top secret formula (that in the process she used every utensil in the kitchen was neither here nor there). The net result, however, never varied;

whatever the dish had started out as, it ended up tasting of nothing. No wonder Bernie smothered everything he ate with tomato ketchup. What was more, like many bad cooks, Nell seemed quite unaware of her lack of ability, and would hover anxiously over Bet's somewhat haphazard but effective efforts with cries of 'Surely you should use the scales, Mum, you'll never get the right consistency like that!' – causing Bet to shut her eyes, think of England, and pray that she wouldn't give way to the impulse to take her darling daughter by her pretty, plump shoulders and shake her until her teeth rattled. When the explosion eventually came, however, it wasn't over the food, but the time at which they all sat down to eat it.

It had been decided before the Sparsworths took up residence that when they did, Bet and Nell would share the cooking on a rota basis; one week Nell, one week Bet; at least until Nell started working when, as Bernie put it, a certain amount of re-scheduling would have to be done – i.e. Bet would do it all. This arrangement had one basic snag. Throughout the Sparsworths' married life Bernie had sat down to his evening meal at six-thirty sharp. This was the time at which he had always eaten it, as had his Dad before him, and this was the time at which he wished to continue to eat it. Bet, on the other hand, throughout her married life had invariably organised family supper for seven-thirty, as had her mother before her, and during her week as duty cook she resolutely refused to have the meal on the table a moment earlier. Hints from Bernie along the lines of 'Need any help, Mrs B.?' or 'Gracious, is that the time. I'm so hungry I could eat a house, only had a cheese and pickle sandwich at dinner time,' had no effect on her whatever, she simply went on sipping her pre-prandial glass of sherry. Matters eventually came to a head when Bet, arriving in the kitchen one evening to make a start on the vegetables, found a box of frozen chips thawing in the sink, a saucepan of baked beans bubbling away on the Rayburn, and her daughter frying beefburgers. When asked what the hell she thought she was up to, Nell, very pink in the face, said she was cooking Bernie's tea. She was sorry if she was in the way, but as Bernie was the household's sole breadwinner, she didn't see why he should be kept waiting for hours for his evening meal, and anyway she (Nell) was fed up with missing 'Coronation Street'.

Then the fat was in the fire! Tears and recriminations (Nell), invective (Bet), oil on troubled waters (Bernie) — mercifully Diz was out to supper with a school friend — during which the beefburgers got burned, nobody watched 'Coronation Street', and nobody had so much as a slice of bread until well past nine o'clock when, worn out with shouting and faint from lack of food, the protagonists collapsed in a heap and decided to call it a day. Embraces and tearful apologies followed, giggles too on the part of Bet and Nell — Bernie didn't seem to think it all that funny. As at the conclusion of most battles, the upshot was a compromise. Bet agreed to put back the evening meal to six forty-five, and Nell and Bernie would eat on their own at weekends, except for Sunday lunch which Bet would cook unless otherwise arranged. On the whole, give or take the odd hiccup, this arrangement had worked pretty well. Bet still cringed at the sight of Bernie's battery of sauce bottles, and Bernie still, no doubt, moaned to his wife about Bet's liberal use of garlic — but one couldn't expect miracles, and on the whole, in that department at least, things weren't too bad.

The real trouble, as far as Bet was concerned, was the loneliness. Stupidly, she had simply not catered for this. She'd accepted, of course, the reality of missing Miles; there would be no escape from that, she knew only too well. But this sense of isolation was something altogether different, and not what she'd hoped for when she made her great decison to move to Suffolk. Indeed, once at the Rectory she'd seen herself as the centre of a busy household, meeting new people, making jam for the W.I., genning up on local history. Even, perhaps giving the occasional modest cocktail party such as she remembered her parents giving at their retirement cottage in Devon in the long ago days before she and Miles were married. But somehow things hadn't turned out like that. But then life never did turn out the way you thought it would, did it? Perhaps it would have helped if she'd been able to drive. Miles had always done the driving, there never seemed to be any need for her to learn. Or perhaps when the Redfords moved in things would get better. But in a way she dreaded their coming.

Not that she was jealous of Pol — or Nell for that matter. Under no circumstances would she have wanted to be married to either Pete or Bernie. But one could not escape the fact that, of the three females living at Hopton Rectory, Bet Brandon would be the odd one out.

So, there it was; after four months she'd made no friends, apart from Miss White at the Post Office and the ubiquitous Mr Bone. There had been one caller, the Rev. Snately, their peripatetic vicar, but it was no use pretending his visit had been a success because it hadn't. Mr Snately was based at Upton Tye, a village a few miles to the east of Hopton, Hopton church having become part of a multiple parish. Being part of a multiple parish meant that three Sundays out of four the church remained its weekday self, empty, damp and shuttered, with only the chirp of a trapped bird in the chancel or a scuffling of mice in the pews to break the silence. Bet knew; she ventured there quite often; had even put her name down as a potential flower-arranger for the vases on the altar, but no one had taken up her offer.

It was freezing cold in the sitting-room the day Mr Snately called, she was out of instant coffee and had been compelled to offer him Bovril, which he plainly disliked. He was very old and very deaf, and they had little to say to each other. In the end he only stayed ten minutes, driving away in his little Morris 1000, wrapped in his thick winter overcoat and looking like some sad old toad.

But it wasn't during the day, when she really was alone, that Bet's sense of isolation bit most deeply. It was in the evening when the children were at home and, supper over, she would retire alone to her sitting-room, shut the door behind her and try not to listen to their excited chatter, as under Bernie's supervision, they sought to bring the old house back to life. It was then that loneliness, like a damp overcoat, wrapped itself around her, and she truly believed she would never feel properly alive again.

There were, of course, compensations. There always were, weren't there, if you looked for them carefully enough? Bet's compensation was the garden. Enormous — much too big for her to cope with, really — wild, mesmeric, totally enchanting and totally time-consuming. She'd had a bit of help with it; a

24

friend of Mr Bone's came one Sunday with his rotovator and turned in the walled vegetable garden (he'd managed to tear out several horseradish plants, a couple of crowns of rhubarb and a plant Bet couldn't put a name to, but was pretty sure was rather rare; no matter, it was a tremendous help all the same), the two boys had cut and raked the lawn and dug out the small forest of unwanted saplings, and Nell, with infinite care and thoroughness, had weeded the rockery. That in doing so she had pulled out most of the things Bet wished to keep and left most of the weeds, was neither here nor there. But despite all this Bet remained undisputed queen of the garden; it was her domain, and in it her will was law.

In the long, soft, autumn days following her and Diz's arrival at the Rectory, she had worked away at the tangled borders for hours on end, planting, dividing, planning, bringing them back to order, back to life. And this occupied her so completely that while she was doing it she found to her surprise that she forgot Miles and her loneliness, forgot even the cataclysmic disruption of the settled existence she had known for so long. She seemed to become a different person, altogether simpler, more self-reliant. At peace in her solitariness, she knelt on the wet ground, her fingernails black with earth and mud on her knees, talking to Tib, talking to herself, dreaming . . .

There was another aspect of the garden she'd grown to love, the verandah. The verandah, Edwardian in design, lay along the south side of the house, facing on to what had already become known as the croquet lawn − Diz, rummaging in the little room behind the stables one wet afternoon, had come across a box of ancient croquet mallets, complete with six hoops and a battered ball. As winters went in that part of the world, it hadn't been particularly cold so far − only the house and Bet's soul were cold − and the verandah, built to trap any sun there might be, was a wonderfully pleasant place to sit and drink one's after-lunch coffee, even if one did have to be muffled in rugs, gloves and a woolly hat. At one end of it a wisteria twined itself in and out of the wrought-iron pillars supporting the roof, at the other, bare ropes of *Clematis montana* and a rampant, viciously spiked Albertine rose formed a woody screen through which gleamed

25

the pale gold sprays of winter-flowering jasmine. Alas part of the Redford domain, the verandah was already scheduled for complete refurbishment; the faded Edwardiana, so much loved by Bet, was shortly to be replaced by sensible, sliding patio doors, double glazing, and all the very latest in designer garden furniture. But meanwhile, enjoying it while she still could, Bet would lie back on the one remaining basket chair, watching the smoke from her cigarette curl up into the misty recesses of a now defunct Virginia creeper, and dream of Edwardian tennis parties long ago. Scrumptious teas with brown-bread ices, cucumber sandwiches and damp seed cake, served by a pretty parlourmaid with streamers in her cap. Men in flannels with ties round their waists, girls in white dresses and bandeaus. Cries of 'Rippin' shot, Angela', 'Well played there, Bertie', echoing round the garden; the smell of full-blown roses, fresh cut grass, warm strawberries . . .

It was while day-dreaming in this way that Bet would sometimes become aware again of that inexplicable upsurge of excitement she had experienced that first day at the Rectory; but it never lasted long, and all too soon would be extinguished by the mundane reality of her daily life. Headlights turning in at the yard gate, car doors slamming, voices . . . 'Mum, can you put supper forward, we've collected that stuff for insulating the roof and we want to get as much done tonight as we can' (Diz). 'I couldn't get the fish, Mum. I had to type a last-minute brief for Mr Slade and only had twenty minutes for lunch. There simply wasn't time to get to the market. Will fish fingers do?' (Nell). 'Sorry, Mrs B.' (Bernie) 'but I'll have to turn the electric off for a bit after supper. Shouldn't be too long, but I want to do those plugs.'

It was through Diz that she first heard of the Westovers of Hopton Manor. Bernie and Diz made regular visits to the Jolly Waggoner, their local pub, and while there, usually managed to pick up some quite useful items of village gossip. That this worked both ways, so that they in their turn passed on some choice titbits about life at the Rectory, Bet didn't doubt; in fact it probably accounted for the odd supicious glance she received while waiting to be served in the village shop, or boarding the twice-weekly bus to Stourwick. And might even account, who knew, for her name being omitted from the flower-arranging roster. Be that as it may, the Westovers were, apparently, the local lords of the manor. At one time they had owned a sizable chunk of the surrounding countryside, including the village itself.

Their seat was Hopton Manor — about three miles from the village on the Stourwick road — and had been since the time of Elizabeth I. Like most old families, they'd had their ups and downs. In fact they had been going downhill pretty fast by the time the nineteenth century came along, until old Saltpeter Westover providentially invented a patent cure for constipation in horses, called it Hopton's Elixir, marketed the stuff all over the Empire and re-founded the family fortunes. Now, however, they were down to their last 750 acres, and according to a Mr Jarman, who appeared to be an authority, the manor itself was in none too good a shape. The present incumbent, so Mr Jarman said, was a woman ('The old man, 'e 'ad no boys'), one Cynthia Westover. Ms Westover, unmarried although well on in her forties, was said to be rather plain, rather tough, combined farming with horse breeding, and was considered by the village to be a good sort. Under her somewhat haphazard rule, life at Hopton Manor continued to maintain that necessary flavour of feudalism spiced with the bizarre (Spanish manservant, alcoholic house parties and assorted skeletons in the cupboard) deemed essential by the indigenous inhabitants of Hopton if the Westover family wished to continue to retain its status as their feudal overlord.

'You see, Mum' — for once Diz was actually helping with the washing-up — 'from an anthropological point of view, Suffolk is quite extraordinarily interesting. Because of its geographical position — out on a limb sticking into the North Sea — the Industrial Revolution simply passed it by. As a result, in the rural areas like Hopton you still get these rigid class-distinctions. Nothing's ever happened to break them up. Anyone who didn't like it emigrated yonks ago, and the ones that remain don't want any change. Did you know that for years Suffolk had the highest incest rate in the country?'

'No,' Bet said, handing back a plate still liberally coated in egg yolk, 'but even I can see it isn't Hampstead.'

27

Chapter Three

What with one thing and another, in the end the Redfords didn't move in until the first week in February. Three days beforehand Pete dropped his bombshell. He would, he said, be unable to get away on The Day until early evening. This was gloomy news indeed and surely a recipe for disaster, making as it did a complete nonsense of all their carefully laid plans. But there it was; nothing, he told them, could be done about it; an emergency meeting of the Top Ten must take precedence over everything else – and he hinted that share prices would tumble and the economy breakdown if he failed to turn up at it. Privately Bet took all this with a pinch of salt, but wisely held her peace.

'Have you ever heard of anything so inconsiderate!' Pol wailed over the phone. 'God knows, he does little enough, you would have thought he could have torn himself away from the office for this one day. But of course, as you know only too well, Bet, his home and his wife have always been way down on Pete's list of priorities.'

From her end Bet made a few compassionate noises, but in truth found it hard to be entirely sympathetic. Why did her sister have to moan so much? However, deciding on balance to assume the somewhat uncharacteristic role of peace-maker – what had Bernie said? we must start as we mean to go on – she put on her soothing-little-sister voice and said What about Diz taking the day off from college to give moral support? She knew perfectly well he would be doing this anyway – he wouldn't have missed the move for anything – but it seemed politic to appear to be making some sacrifice in

28

the cause of the Redfords' future comfort.

The furniture van from London being scheduled for eight-thirty a.m., Pol duly arrived the evening before. All through the previous week a steady stream of delivery men had called at the Rectory, someone had come to lay carpets, and on Monday the kitchen units arrived — teak and copper and costing almost as much as the house itself. Each evening Nell, Bernie and Diz would inspect the new arrivals, mostly with scorn and ribald laughter, but also, Bet suspected, in Nell and Bernie's case, with considerable envy. She herself, creeping in later when no one was about, couldn't help admitting the kitchen was pretty impressive, though the carpets weren't really her cup of tea and some of the light fittings she thought quite frightful. The problem of Pol's twice-weekly daily had been solved without the help of old Monty Cornwall or his wife. A Christine Barnet, young, lively and sensible — rather plain, too, which was an asset with Pete around — had appeared one morning in answer to Bet's notice, and at what seemed, in comparison with Hampstead, an incredibly reasonable hourly rate, had agreed to clean the Redfords' part of the house. Mrs Barnet, born and bred in Hopton, was one of the younger members of a vast family called Kettle, whose tentacles apparently stretched as far as Stourwick, and Bet was fairly sure that the day after Christine's visits, the smallest happenings at the Rectory would be the main topic at breakfast tables throughout the county. All the same, Christine was a nice girl, and Bet hoped — but doubted — that Pol would be suitably grateful for her assistance.

On the evening of Pol's arrival, Pol and Bet sat in Bet's kitchen; Diz was upstairs working and the Sparsworths were out somewhere. 'Absolutely typical,' Pol said. 'The one moment in our entire marriage when I really need Pete, he isn't here.' Bet, unable to stop herself, gave a derisive snort. It worked. 'Oh God, I'm sorry, Bet, I'm always moaning, and you haven't anyone to moan about. But P. is such a bore, I can't help it.'

'Don't mind me, I'm used to it.' Bet knew she sounded waspish, but too bad. 'If you find Pete such a bore, why on earth are you so annoyed he won't be here tomorrow?'

'You don't understand, do you? You never did. Just

because you thought Miles was perfect — I've had doubts on that score myself, and so have quite a few other people — you think everyone else's husband must be the same.'

For a moment the desire to pull her sister's beautifully cut, beautifully blow-dried blonde hair almost overcame Bet, but sense prevailed. 'Look, Pol, don't let's quarrel, it's so silly. Here we are in this lovely old house, living under the same roof for the first time in nearly thirty years' — Pol winced — 'do let's try and make a go of it. I mean, even without Pete it'll be fun seeing how all your things go. And Diz will be here to help. He can be a bit tiresome, I know, but he can be funny too. Then there's . . . '

To her horror, she suddenly became aware that Pol was about to burst into tears. Ignoring the still, small, anarchic voice inside her that proclaimed *she* was the one who should be crying, *she* was the one who had something to cry about, not her selfish sister, she gently stroked Pol's hand as she'd so often done when Pol was a little girl. 'Come on, Polly-Wolly, let's have a drink, and then we'll go upstairs and have another look at your bedroom.'

It seemed to do the trick. Her sister closed her eyes, opened them again, blew her nose on a handy Kleenex, smiled bravely and reached for the gin bottle.

Despite Pete's absence, the day went smoothly. The furniture van turned smartly in at the gate at eight-thirty on the dot, the two removal men, unlike their predecessors, proving extremely competent. What was more, they seemed delighted with Pol's tip, which turned out to be precisely half what Bet had given her two. But then she wasn't used to tipping, was she? Miles had always done that . . .

Pete arrived soon after five. They were all seated round Bet's kitchen table — the Sparsworths home early in honour of the occasion — having a much needed cup of tea. It had been decided not to use Pol's kitchen, splendid though this was, its designer having palpably not catered for people sitting down in it. The two spindly chairs provided were more suited to a smart cocktail bar in Mayfair, or even a smart kindergarten, than for weary people to rest their bottoms on.

'Just as we've finished. One might have known,' Pol said as Pete's Aston Martin purred to a halt outside the kitchen window. He appeared a moment later, smiling sheepishly, his arms full of bottles of champagne. 'Here you all are then. How goes it?'

'Fine.' Pol offered a frosty cheek. 'No thanks to you. Bet and Diz have been splendid, I simply don't know what I would have done without them.'

'But Bet always is quite splendid, aren't you, my duck.' Pete kissed his sister-in-law on the lips, giving her a slightly unnecessary squeeze at the same time. 'Now then, you can pour that there slop you're drinking down the sink and get these 'ere bottles open. Come on, Bet, where are your champagne glasses? We might as well celebrate in style. And after that your Uncle Pete is taking you all out to dinner.'

Pol gave her hair a pat and fiddled with her pearls. She'd insisted on wearing her pearls despite the unsuitability of the occasion, claiming, perhaps rightly, that they were safer round her neck than anywhere else. 'That, if I may say so, is the first good idea you've had in weeks. By the way, did you remember to bring my electric blanket?'

'Of course I did. You know your old husband never forgets anything. That's why I'm a bit late, I had to go all the way back to Chelsea to collect it.' With the flourish of an expert, he twisted the champagne cork. 'Now then, fill up your glasses and let's go on a tour of inspection.'

Dear Pete, thought Bet, she did have to admit he had his points.

Three hours and several bottles of champagne later, the entire party set out in search of somewhere to eat, the Redfords and Bet in the Aston Martin and the other three in Bernie's Renault. After much discussion they had decided to try a new place, recently opened, so Pete told them, by a cousin of old Fruity Nicholson's. 'I hope you don't mind my asking, Uncle Pete, but who's Fruity Nicholson? I'd no idea there were still people around called Fruity — it's so frightfully twenties, isn't it?' Bet looked at Diz sharply; lucky there was no college tomorrow, he'd had three glasses of champagne already.

'Fruity Nicholson?' Pete poured himself another drink, 'marvellous old boy, some sort of relative of Monty Cornwall's.'

'He had to be,' Nell whispered to her husband.

'Lives in a castle complete with tower, drawbridge, the lot, only a few miles from here. The place was built by some Victorian jam manufacturer, so Fruity said. Well, I asked him if he knew of anywhere decent to eat out in this neck of the woods, and he mentioned that a cousin of his had recently opened a restaurant. The Donkey's Shoe at Upton Lyttel — superb cooking, so he'd heard, and not too pricey either. Unless anyone else has any other ideas, I thought it might be a good plan if we tried it tonight.'

No one had any other ideas, a Berni Inn in Stourwick on Diz's birthday was so far the sum total of their experience of eating out locally. Bernie did tentatively suggest The George at Stotleigh, it being so near and time getting on, but his suggestion met with little response. 'I think we all deserve something a little better than overdone steak and frozen chips, Bernie dear,' Pol said, smiling kindly at him. Bernie was not to be patronised. 'Well, I just thought this Donkey's Shoe, or whatever it's called, might be difficult to get into on a Friday night, that's all. I mean, as we haven't booked — '

'No need to worry about that! Fruity said just to mention his name at the door — no problem.'

'Still, it might be wiser just to check ... Oh, never mind.' Bernie subsided into sulky silence. Nell squeezed his hand.

As things turned out, it was past eight-thirty by the time they arrived at Upton Lyttel, since it was considerably further away from Hopton than they'd been led to suppose, and a number of wrong turnings were taken en route. Already the atmosphere in the Redford car, initially mellow, had begun to deteriorate. All were tired, and looking forward to relaxing in the ambience of Fruity Nicholson's cousin's eatery.

Their first sight of the village was not propitious, a double line of parked cars down the main street bearing witness to the popularity of the restaurant, which itself boasted a car park capable of taking only ten vehicles. However, by a stroke of luck some early diners were just leaving as Pete hovered uncertainly in the middle of the road, and he was able to squeeze into the gap left by their car. Bernie, not so lucky, was forced to continue on down the village street for another quarter of a mile.

32

'Come on, girls, I'm starving even if you aren't.' Pete, apparently oblivious to the obvious fact that the place was full, walked purposefully towards what appeared to be a huge converted tithe barn. The noise was deafening. Fruity's cousin had hit the jackpot; there was no doubt that the Donkey's Shoe was the 'in' place to visit on a Friday night.

'Table for six, dear? You must be joking.' A young man attired in a sketchy imitation of an eighteenth-century shepherd's outfit peered at them through a bundle of stuffed rabbits and a stook of plastic corn. 'The best I can do is the annexe. Never mind, you'll be able to watch Clement at his forge and there's bags of atmosphere. Go straight through, past the trelliswork, turn right at the sheep dip — you can't miss it. You may have to wait a bit for your order, mind, we're rushed off our feet tonight.' He vanished into the murk. Grim-faced, they pushed their way down the seething barn, found what they assumed was the sheep dip, turned right at it, and at long last came upon their vacant table. The reason for it being vacant on such a busy evening now became blindingly obvious: not only was it placed practically underneath the loudspeaker — at that moment blasting out a rock version of 'Gathering Peascods' — but it backed on to Clement's forge.

For a moment or two they sat in stunned silence. In any case, the din was such that in order to be heard at all one was compelled to shout like the captain of a ship in a Force 8 gale, and it was all too dreadfully plain, that Fruity's name had not worked its expected magic. Bet, already floating in a happy, alcoholic hinterland, was enjoying herself enormously. She felt like a child on a birthday treat; each new disaster befalling the grown-ups was an added bonus. She would feel like death in the morning, but who cared. The music changed to 'Greensleeves' and a laconic shepherdess loomed. 'Anything to drink while you wait?' she asked sharply, and shoved a jumbo-sized bill of fare into Pete's nerveless hands. 'Three gin and tonics,' he bawled. 'We can't order yet, the rest of our party — '

'You'll have to get a move on, the kitchen closes at ten.'

'Oh. Oh dear.' Pete looked wildly round. Pol watched him, smiling sweetly, the heat from Clement's forge causing the sweat to trickle gently down her perfectly made-up face.

There was another deafening pause, then Bet saw them. Bernie led the way, purposeful, efficient, his face a mask, followed by her two: Diz, gesticulating wildly, and Nell, puce in the face with supressed giggles. Smiling dreamily, Bet watched them, and for one long, marvellous moment her love for them enveloped her entirely; stupid tears came into her eyes and there was a lump in her throat. How lucky she really was. And thank God for Pete, too, what would they do without him?

Diz hurried forward, one hand outstretched. 'Mr Stanley, I presume, my name's Livingstone, David Livingstone, and I've walked across two continents to find you.'

'All-right, all-right, joke over. Anyway, wasn't it the other way round? I mean, wasn't it Stanley who went to look for Livingstone, I always thought −'

'Pete, it may have escaped your notice, but we've been told by the waitress' − Pol glanced contemptuously at the scowling shepherdess − 'that the kitchens close at ten. If we don't make our orders quickly we shan't get anything to eat at all, although heaven knows, in a place like this one shudders to think what it will be like if we do.'

In the end they opted for leek soup and venison steaks, there being little left to choose anyway. The food, when it finally arrived, turned out to be tasteless, the bill enormous. 'Ninety per cent ambience and ten per cent nutrition,' Diz told them, but by that time they were all too exhausted to care.

'I suppose I shall have to drive, you're in no condition to do so.' Pol brushed past Pete and briskly led the way out of the still-humming restaurant into the cold night air. 'Would you mind awfully, ducky, I am most frightfully tired, it seems to have been one hell of a long day.' The others departed to look for Bernie's car, wandering down the village street, arms linked, chanting some Beatles' song from the sixties.

Pete climbed ponderously into the back of the Aston Martin and promptly went to sleep. Pol expertly fastened her seat belt, started the engine, and neatly reversed into the car behind. Pete woke with a jerk. 'What's happened, darling? What have you −?'

'I should think that was fairly obvious, she's driven into the front of my car, the stupid cow.' A man's face thrust itself through the car window, hair on end, eyes blazing. Beelzebub himself!, Bet, still in her trance, looked at the man with wondering eyes.

'Look here, I'm extremely sorry, but there's no earthly need to insult my wife; she's a very competent driver, it must have been the frost on the rear window – '

'I don't care a tinker's fart what it was. If you had an ounce of sense between you, someone would have thought of cleaning it.'

'Call the police at once, Pete. I am not going to be insulted like this.'

'For heaven's sake, belt up, ducky. What d'you imagine the police can do? Look, I'm sure we can settle things amicably and of course I accept full liability. I'll just pop out and we can have a dekko at the damage.'

Considering his condition, Pete's dignity was impressive. The face withdrew from the window and for an instant Bet saw its owner quite clearly under the street lamp. Medium height, shorter than Pete; but then most people were, for Pete was a giant, with broad shoulders (nice), and dark curly hair turning to grey (even nicer). The man's expression was still diabolical, but with those slanting eyebrows it could not be anything else. The mouth was a bit on the sensual side, but surprisingly gentle for such a satanic-looking individual, and she'd always liked men with cleft chins. Actually, he looked a bit foreign; Spanish perhaps, or possibly Italian; although this impression was belied by the fact that when he opened his mouth, the tone of voice and accent were unmistakably those of an upper-crust Englishman, and a pretty arrogant upper-crust Englishman at that.

The two men disappeared from view.

A few minutes later Pete returned, smiling genially. 'Not to worry. Only smashed the glass on the chap's headlight, could have been much worse. I gave him a cheque for fifty pounds to cover any damage, but it won't come near that. We don't want the insurance boys involved unnecessarily.'

'Are you saying you gave that frightful man fifty pounds for insulting me? Did you hear what he called me, Pete, did you hear ...?' But Pete was asleep again.

* * *

35

Sunday evening. An empty house, the children at a rock concert in Stourwick, Bet alone by the fire considering her weekend. Somewhat surprisingly, it had been rather fun. But then as she seemed to have spent a large part of it in an alcoholic haze, it could hardly be counted as a taste of things to come. Did the Redfords always drink like that, or only on special occasions? It would be interesting to find out.

She'd seen them off back to London an hour ago, amidst a hail of last-minute instructions from Pol for herself and Christine Barnet. She had little intention of carrying out hers, and Christine Barnet could decide for herself. After they'd gone, she'd poached herself an egg and retired to her sitting-room with Parson Woodforde's Diaries and the remains of the Sunday newspapers. Having consumed the egg and given Tib the toast crusts, she found she couldn't be bothered to read the papers — it was never the same reading the Sunday papers at the end of the day, the impetus had somehow gone — and she was beginning to get a bit fed up with Parson Woodforde's incessant eating. So she just sat back in Miles's chair (hers now) with her feet on a stool, looking into the fire and listening to the silence. She was, she thought, beginning rather to like silence. Silence as an entity was something she'd never been aware of before; until now her life hadn't been noisy exactly, or at least she didn't think it had, it was just that she couldn't remember silence. Was she becoming a recluse? She sipped her coffee and saw herself a few years from now: a mysterious figure, rarely glimpsed by anyone outside her family, pottering around in shapeless tweeds and a moth-eaten cardigan, muttering to herself; a witch weaving spells in her garden, drinking her tot of medicinal whisky of an evening. 'My mother doesn't go out much, actually. She's rather shy . . .' The vision made her giggle so much that she upset her coffee and even managed to rouse Tib from his hearthrug lethargy.

It was while she was mopping up the spilled coffee that, without warning, a man's face came into her mind. The picture was as clear as a black and white photograph, and the face belonged to the angry man in the car park on Friday evening. The man whose car Pol had backed into, the man who'd actually had the temerity to call her sister a stupid cow.

She knew now who the face reminded her of; not Beelzebub, but that portrait of Cosimo Medici in Florence. She couldn't remember who had painted the portrait but she knew it was in the Uffizi. She and Miles had seen it on that holiday in Italy years ago, before the children were born. She'd kept wanting to go back and have another look at it. 'Fancy him, darling?' Miles had said, 'he looks a bit supercilious to me.'

'Of course I don't, you ass,' she'd said, squeezing his hand, but of course she had. And Miles, who knew everything, must have known she had, because on her next birthday he gave her a postcard of the portrait with *Sorry I can't compete, darling. Never mind, Medicis can be a bit dodgy, you're much better off with a civil servant* written on the back. She'd kept that card for years; it might even still be around somewhere, perhaps she'd have a look for it tomorrow.

But how very odd to find Cosimo Medici in a Suffolk car park.

Tib woke up and leaned his head against her knee and she gently stroked his ears in the way she knew he loved. Perhaps ... to be absolutely honest ... she wasn't ready to become a recluse quite yet ...

'Well, ducky, and what did you think of it all?' Pete and Pol were driving through the wet dark towards London and civilization. Pol, who'd been half-asleep, opened her eyes and yawned. 'Of course, there are a hundred things that still need sorting out – that wretched dog of Bet's for a start. And I'm not sure if I can live with that colour in the kitchen; it looked marvellous in the photo, but now –'

'I didn't mean that. What I meant was, how d'you like it in principle? Is it going to work? I know dinner on Friday evening was a bit of a shambles, but at least it gave the kids a laugh.'

'Rather an expensive method of amusing the children! It would have been cheaper for you to have simply fallen flat on your face.'

'Don't be like that, ducky, you know what I mean. And don't worry, next time I see old Fruity I shan't hesitate to tell him exactly what I think of his cousin's bloody eatery – the Donkey's Shoe, my arse!'

'There's no need to be coarse, you know I don't like it. It's odd how being with Bet always seems to have that effect on you. Heaven knows why — she and Miles were always so fearfully proper.'

Pete smiled, and nipped smartly into the outside lane to overtake a couple of lorries.

'Pol?'

'Umm?'

'There's something I've always wondered about Bet.'

'Umm?'

'Has she ever . . . well, ever . . .? Apart from old Miles, that is. I mean — '

'I know perfectly well what you mean, and quite frankly it isn't any of your business. But if the question is keeping you awake at night, I'm fairly sure the answer is No, she hasn't.'

Pete whistled and was silent for a minute. Then, 'That's what I thought you'd say. All the same, quite a surprise when you come to think of it . . . a women like Bet.'

Nell Sparsworth lay on her back in bed, watching her husband undress. She loved every square inch of him; it was impossible, she thought, to love anyone so much.

Bernie folded his clothes neatly on a chair, took off his digital watch and climbed into bed beside her. He gently nuzzled her ear. 'Darling, darling little Nell, aren't you the luckiest girl in the world to have me as a husband.'

Nell buried her head in his chest. 'I am the luckiest girl in the world. I am, I am, I am . . .'

Diz lay on his back in his narrow bed, hands together as though in prayer, and tried not to listen to the noises coming from next door. He was practising his nightly meditation; his latest thing. Tonight, however, somehow he found it rather hard to concentrate. Perhaps he'd give it a miss; try again tomorrow night . . .

He fell asleep.

Chapter Four

Saturday morning, with everyone in a mood. Bet, doling out breakfast, threw a stone into troubled waters. 'You'd better all mind your ps and qs this weekend. Next Door are entertaining their first house guests — an American couple by the name of Hackenbit. Your Aunt Pol says Mr H. is something important on the New York Stock Exchange, so will we keep the dog under control and not hang out washing in the back yard.'

It was several weeks, now, since the Redfords had moved in, and already a clump of real, wild daffodils had appeared in the field beyond the church, dog violets and primroses straggled under the wall by the stables, and Bet had sown her first batch of broad beans. Little had been seen of the Redfords since they took possession of their part of the Rectory. Indeed, they'd only been down once, and then were out most of the time. 'Making contact with the local mafioso, no doubt,' Bernie, wearing his I-told-you-so expression, informed his wife. Privately Bet wondered whether her sister was perhaps already regretting the easy camaraderie of that first weekend, and had decided in future to adopt a slightly lower profile in her dealings with herself and the Sparsworths.

'If the Hackenbits are that important we shall be *persona non grata* anyway, so why bother?' Bernie was the first to rise to Bet's bait. 'There's no need to show off your Latin, Bern, it doesn't impress me and the women don't understand anyway.' Diz watched his brother-in-law cut decisively into the glistening fried egg on his loaded plate and wait while the yolk ran tantalisingly over the crisp bacon surrounding it

39

before transferring a fork-load to his mouth. His own meagre breakfast – part of his meditation kick – consisted of a handful of bran and a few raisins, and was far from appetising.

'You're both wrong,' Bet said, watching a shaft of sun slant through the kitchen window and light up the honey-coloured mug of early wallflowers she had placed on the dresser – she sometimes wondered why she bothered. 'I got an O-Level in Latin and Aunt Pol has invited us all to meet them for a drink in the George at lunchtime today.'

'Count me out, then. I'm playing football this afternoon and the last thing I want is a drinking session with the Redfords, even if it does mean meeting influential Americans.' Bernie wiped the egg from his moustache and turned back to his *Daily Mail*.

'Darling please! We shan't be able to get there if you don't come, and you promised to drive Mum to Stotleigh today so she could get some of those home-made cakes in that lovely baker's – she can't get there during the week, there's no bus. Don't be such a killjoy. You don't have to drink if you don't want to.'

'Want to bet, with Uncle Pete around?'

'Oh shut up, Diz, can't you keep your interfering nose out of it for once; you're such a stirrer. Honestly, I often think you're responsible for almost every row we have in this family . . .'

But in the end they all went. Bernie hated himself for giving in, but despite his publicly avowed disapproval of the Redford lifestyle, to his own considerable annoyance he found he could never resist joining in any scheme with which they were connected. And he had to admit they had their uses. He had even managed to raise a smile from his manager – no mean feat – with the story of the ill-fated evening at the Donkey's Shoe; and hadn't he heard somewhere that Gerry Hackenbit was connected with some big insurance syndicate in the States?

By the time they arrived at The George, the car park was already jammed and Bet was in one of her depressions. These, much rarer now, were usually triggered by some minor mishap she couldn't even remember afterwards. While they lasted, all the ills of her single state would merge together in one horrendous blurr, leaving her with one desire only, and that was to sit in a corner with a sack over her head and never speak to anyone again. What was more, she felt a headache coming on.

Like its car park, The George, an old market-place pub lately transformed into the brewery's idea of an Elizabethan hostelry, was packed, and for a moment, as they tried to penetrate the gloom of the Merrie England Cocktail Lounge, they were unable to see anything. Then Diz managed to pick out Pete among the throng round the bar, looking hearty in an expensive fisherman's jersey and cavalry twill trousers. 'Ah, here you all are. Meet my good friend, Gerry – Pol and Laurie are over there in the corner.' He pointed a vague finger.

They found Pol seated under a rather venomous-looking eighteenth-century fowling-piece, looking just right in perfectly-cut tweed slacks and a silk shirt, her hair the colour of spun gold. Beside her was Laurie Hackenbit, a blue-rinsed matron of uncertain age liberally sprinkled with costume jewellery, including a gold charm-bracelet which tinkled prettily every time she moved her beautifully manicured hands. The sight of them both, so animated and so charming, served only – if that were possible – to deepen Bet's depression.

Actually, Pol was feeling rather bored. She had to admit the Hackenbits were a little on the dull side ... and she did wish American men wouldn't wear those frightful tartan trousers. Bet, she could see at a glance, was in one of her moods, so there would be no help from that quarter.

'Now tell me, Polly, would you say those wonderful old beams were once part of a ship? I just think that's such a lovely idea.' Pol looked at Bet. Surely she could at least make *some* effort? Then she noticed to her horror that Diz was about to go into his Groucho Marx impression. 'Pete,' she shouted in despair, 'hurry up with our drinks, it's all very well for you.'

At that precise moment Bet saw him again; the cross man from the car park. She was right, he did look like Cosimo de Medici. He was leaning against the bar at the far end of the room, and formed part of a small, interesting group. There was a large, horsey lady with a carrying, county voice, who was smoking a small cheroot and had a tweed hat smashed down on her untidy blonde-streaked hair; there was a dark girl wearing jeans and a T-shirt with 'Save our Local Heritage' emblazoned across the front; and there was a beefy young man who was possibly a vet, certainly a member of the local Young Farmers and a Young Conservative. On balance it seemed a rather unlikely set of people for the cross man to be drinking with, but of course it was no business of Bet's. He still looked cross, but this time, bored as well. He must have sensed she was looking at him, as he turned round suddenly and their eyes met. It was then she discovered that not only did he look like the protrait of Cosimo de Medici, but he had the same effect on her too. The cross man, as though aware of her reaction, raised his glass and winked.

'I say, I've just seen the chap you backed into the other night.' Pete loomed. 'Still looks pretty fed up to me. He's with that group over there — woman with the voice and the hat.' Everyone looked; the Hackenbits were rather pleased at this apparent fall from grace on the part of their hostess, her social poise until now had seem impregnable. The cross man, meeting their combined gaze from his end of the bar, bowed slightly, in the manner of an actor acknowledging applause, and returned to his drink.

'Oh my, Polly, that must have been just so embarrassing —'

'A storm in a teacup, actually, I can't think why Pete had to bring it up.' And Pol proceeded to give her (slightly bowdlerised) version of the incident in the Donkey's Shoe car park, finishing up with her usual diatribe on current manners. Laurie, energetically shaking her bangles, agreed. The conversation droned on.

At long last Nell rose to her feet — no one else looked as if they were going to. 'We really must be going, my husband's playing football this afternoon.' But by now Bernie didn't want to leave; he'd managed to hold his own pretty well with Gerry and Pete, he thought, even contributed one or two quite valid points to the conversation. Gerry had gone so far as to say that if he and Nell ever visited New York . . .

The crowd had thinned considerably as they made their way towards the Gothic arch that formed the entrance to the Merrie England Cocktail Lounge, but the cross man and his friends were still at the bar. 'I say, aren't you the new people

42

at the Rectory?' The lady in the tweed hat waved her cheroot and addressed them in a voice that could, at a pinch, have been heard in the car park. 'I should have called, but we've been in Bermuda – I'm Cynthia Westover.'

The Rectory party, taken off balance, halted uncertainly, then after a few false starts managed to produce a sort of combined mumble of assent; they were indeed the new people at the Rectory. Ms Westover took a gulp of her pink gin. 'I gather you have a dog. Make sure it doesn't disturb the pheasants, won't you.' And with another wave of her cheroot, she turned back to the beefy, young man. 'You know, Rodders, I'm pretty sure there's woodcock in Tranter's this year . . .' They were dismissed.

They emerged, seething, into the car park. Bernie, scowling, slammed the car door, and fastened his seat-belt with a vicious snap. 'Well, I think I've proved my point! Who says there's no class system in this country any more? Talk about the feudal pyramid – we were just so much dirt under that old cow's feet.'

'Oh, don't be silly, darling, she's just that sort of woman, she didn't mean to be rude.'

'I quite agree she didn't mean to be rude; people like her don't know the meaning of the word. She's so used to being top of the heap in her crappy little world, it never occurs to her even to consider anybody else's feelings.'

'What interests me,' said Diz from the back, 'is how the man who Aunt Pol bumped into fits in. D'you think he's our Cynthia's fancy man?' Precisely the same thought had occurred to his mother, but for some reason she preferred to think otherwise, and throughout the journey home remained uncharacteristically silent, content to let the arguments for and against the classless society rage round her unchecked.

Back at the Rectory, Bernie fired his parting shot before ridding himself of his pent-up aggression on the football field. 'There's one thing we can be sure of, the names of Sparsworth and Brandon will not be appearing on the Westover guest list. I doubt if the Redfords will either, in spite of old Monty Cornwall. After all, Pete does get his money from trade.'

However, for once Bernie was wrong, because only a few days later Bet and the cross man met again.

Chapter Five

It was the day Bet took Tib for his walk in the wood. Tib had a walk every day, he expected it; but, used to running wild on Hampstead Heath, he had grown bored with being marched round the lanes on a lead. – and for that matter, Bet had grown bored with it too. On being applied to, Christine Barnet suggested the wood. It belonged, she said, to the Westovers, but had always been open to the village – the squire was like that. Her gran had done her courting there, and so had many others, and the children still picked the primroses to decorate the church at Easter. The idea of going to the wood excited Bet. She could see it from her bedroom window. Only a field away from the Rectory garden, it crouched along the rim of the hill, witchy, mysterious, its ancient, serpentine edge curling in and out between the chocolate-coloured furrows of the field that bordered it.

It was a cold, still, April day – nearer winter than spring – when they set out, and Bet was just a little nervous by the time they had crossed the field and found the mouth of the bridle path Christine had told her about. There was the same sense of awe as on entering a cathedral, it seemed necessary to tiptoe, keep one's voice down, look about in a kind of wonder. She started down the ride. On either side immensely tall ash trees reared up towards the sky, their bases contorted into a hundred bizarre shapes. And every so often within the labyrinth of trees – rather like coming upon one of those minute piazzas when wandering the streets of an Italian city – there would be a small clearing, in the middle of which stood a large and spreading oak. Wood anemones were scattered over dry, brown leaves in a network of white and green; there were clumps of primroses and the spotted leaves of purple orchids not yet in flower; one could see that later the place would be alive with bluebells.

It was the most beautiful wood Bet had ever been in.

She walked quietly, hardly daring to breathe in the silence, looking up every now and again at the patches of pale sky filtering through the grey tracery of winter-bare branches above her head. At first Tib, also a little in awe of the place, kept close to her heels, but after a while grew bolder, eventually running on ahead so far that she lost sight of him in the maze of trees. Then suddenly a jay flew across the ride in front of her, its harsh, warning cry reminding her of childhood summers in the New Forest; she and Dad crouching together in a hazel bush, watching for red deer.

'Tib? Tib, where are you?' She was feeling nervous again – Little Grey Rabbit all on her own in the Weasel Wood. Then the barking started, and not just Tib either; there was a strange bark as well, and a man's voice shouting – Oh God!

'Tib, come here, you bastard, before I murder you!' She started to run; round a bend in the path, boots squelching in the muddy ruts, breath coming in short, sharp gasps. Was it the Westovers' keeper? Would he shoot Tib? God, what a fool she'd been to let him off the lead in the first place, and damn and blast Christine Barnet!

'Look here, you two, if you're going to fight, fight. If not, belt up. I've a hell of a head as it is and ... Good heavens, it's Mrs Brandon! I did so hope we'd meet again and now we have.' From under the branches of a spreading oak the cross man laughed at her. Beside him, eyeball to eyeball, hackles raised, snarling horribly, Tib and a large, hairy, marmalade-coloured dog confronted each other.

'Oh dear, I'm most frightfully sorry. Tib's a complete coward actually, he ... How on earth did you know my name?'

'Hardly very difficult; Hopton isn't Hampstead, you know. And there's no need to apologise, Oxford's to blame as much as yours. Perhaps if we shake hands they'll calm down. They're probably only showing the flag. My name, in case you didn't know, is Simon Morris.'

'I didn't know.' Bet was still fighting for breath. She took off her glove, it had mud on it and there was a hole in the thumb. 'How d'you do,' she said feeling a bit of an idiot. His hand was sharply cold. Did he hold onto hers a little longer than was necessary, or was that her imagination?

'It's worked, look,' Simon said. And it had. The two dogs subsided on to the ground, tongues lolling, looking rather foolish. Whatever else he might be, the cross man was knowledgable about dogs.

'Now that's over, come and sit down. You look quite done in — have you run far?'

'No, of course I haven't, and I'm not in the least done in. I was just worried. I thought Miss Westover had a game-keeper and I ought to have kept Tib on the lead, but Christine Barnet said it was all-right to come to the wood.'

'Christine Kettle that was?'

'Yes, as a matter of fact, but how did you — ?'

'Everyone knows the Kettle family. Christine's mum taught me the facts of life. One Easter holidays it was, and if I remember rightly, I wouldn't believe her. Shame she's run to fat, but then she was a daughter of old Sid Garnham, and all his girls did — run to fat, I mean.'

'You know this part of the world pretty well, then?' Her bottom, balanced precariously on a mossy tree stump, was getting damp, and she was still breathless.

'Pretty well. I was brought up here. Cyn Westover's my cousin.'

'Oh. Oh, I see.'

'You thought I was some sort of gigolo, didn't you — the local squire's toy-boy. Come on, don't be embarrassed, people often think that. I suppose it's because I have that dago look. My Dad was Italian, you see.'

'Cosimo de Medici — I was right!'

'Cosimo what?'

'Oh, it doesn't matter, nothing really . . .'

'Look, you can't suddenly shout 'Cosimo de Medici' and then say it doesn't matter . . .'

Afterwards, although she tried, Bet couldn't remember much of their subsequent conversation. They'd laughed quite a bit — a lot, actually — and she'd told him about Miles and

46

the children and living in Hampstead, she did remember that. She now knew that he was 'loosely connected with advertising', had been largely responsible for that commercial about the box of chocolates dancing with an Airedale ('My chef-d'oevre; perhaps it's time I moved on'), that he was always changing jobs, was unmarried, and that he and Cynthia Westover had been brought up together, his Italian father having died in the war — so he must have told her all that. But how long they spent sitting under the oak tree she'd had no idea — until she had sense to look at her watch and discover to her horror that it was already quarter-past four.

'Heavens, I must go, I should be home by now, putting the stew in the oven, the children will be back soon and — '

'Do you know why they planted oaks in among the ash trees?' She shook her head; she didn't want to go. 'So that when the ash trees are cut and growth begins again, the shade from the oak makes them reach up towards the light instead of branching out. The trees are coppiced a section at a time, and if it's done properly in rotation, you get a continuous supply of usable ash poles throughout the year. The conservation people would love to get their hands on this wood, they say it's a perfect example of coppicing continued without interruption for centuries, and Cyn doesn't look after it properly. They're probably right there, but of course she won't sell. And do you know that at midsummer there are butterfly orchids? Butterfly orchids are greeny-white and rather rare; they only release their scent at dusk, you see they're pollinated by moths and — '

'It's a beautiful, beautiful wood,' she said, 'but I really must go.' And she was suddenly afraid he was going to kiss her.

Afraid?

But he didn't kiss her, he merely patted her on the shoulder. 'Mind how you go, then, Mrs Brandon, and I'd watch out with Tib and the pheasants if I were you.' Then, whistling up Oxford — hopefully digging for rabbits a few yards away — he was gone, leaving Bet looking after him and feeling cheated. Silly, really, considering she was the one who said she had to go.

It was while she was walking across the field of young wheat that divided the rectory garden from the wood that she decided – frankly, she wasn't altogether sure why – she'd not tell the others about her meeting with the cross man. She'd tell about the wood, of course, but . . .

'Checkmate!' Triumphant, Cynthia Westover took a gulp of her brandy and ginger, and smiled across the table at her cousin Simon, who simply looked annoyed. 'Come on, Si, don't sulk, you're a big boy now, remember.'

'You know perfectly well I could beat you with one hand tied behind my back and my eyes shut if I wanted to. I just can't concentrate this evening. Let's turn out the lights and watch the horror movie.'

'Not tonight, my love, I have to be up at six a.m. Rodders is taking me to have a look at that filly. Come on, Ox, up you get, you lazy hound, it's bedtime.' She turfed the sleeping marmalade dog off his nest in the sofa cushions, and then stretched, looking down at the top of Simon's head as he bent to put away the chess men. Then, as one performing some sort of rite, she dribbled the remaining contents of her glass over his hair.

'Oh shut up, Cyn, and leave me alone, I'm not in the mood.'

'Has our Simmy got his black monkey, then? Shall Cyn drive him away? Take him by his long black tail and throw him out of the window – Like This!' She plunged on top of Simon, knocking him off his chair, and they rolled, fighting, on to the carpet.

A log collapsed in the grate, outside an owl hooted, and the dog, Oxford, used to such antics, waited patiently to be let out for his evening run.

Later, upstairs in Cyn's bedroom, Simon smoked a last cigarette and watched his cousin put cream on her face.

'Cyn?'

'Yes, my poppet?'

'Do me a favour?'

'Depends what it is, and please use the ash-tray, Alfonso's getting restive again. He nearly had a fit when Pooh Bah made a mess in the bath last week, and he's started on again about that cousin of his in Madrid who has a restaurant – '

48

'Stop waffling and listen. All I'm asking is — you know you said you thought you'd give a party when sexy Sonia comes to stay next week?'

'You want me to invite that Brandon woman from the Rectory, don't you?'

Simon looked at her with genuine admiration. 'Cyn,' he said, 'you're the cleverest girl in Suffolk, in England, in the world; you know everything and can do anything —'

'Never mind all that, I'm not in the mood. That is what you want, isn't it?'

'Well, I just thought they seemed a bit out of the usual run of retired majors and redundant bank managers with spotty daughters who normally settle round here, that's all.'

'I thought you said the sister was absolutely frightful, the one that ran into you at that ghastly place of Pogo Nicholson's.'

'She wasn't that bad, she just took me by surprise, and the husband's OK; a bit of an ass, I suppose, but then who isn't. Anyway, how did you know I wanted you to ask Mrs Brandon, you only saw her in The George that day.'

'Good God, you twerp, I haven't known you for forty-odd years without being able to see when you fancy someone! Heaven knows, I've had enough experience. But Si, she's not your type. Ex-Hampstead, civil servant's widow; a bit on the arty side, I'd say, by the look of her. She's not in your league, she really isn't.'

'It's got nothing to do with being in my league. I just want to get to know her a little. She's a good-looker, you have to admit that.'

'I'm not admitting anything. She's also several years older than you and has a married daughter and a son of seventeen. Honestly, Si, it's not on, I mean, not for the kind of thing you have in mind.'

'So you're saying you won't ask them, you'll just ignore their existence. Isn't that rather rude? Surely, in your capacity as squire of the village —'

'Balls! Since when, pray, have you ever concerned yourself with my capacity as squire of the village?'

'Don't change the subject. I should have thought it would have been a simple thing to do, just to ask them to a party. If

Sonia's going to be there, the more guests the better; that woman runs through people quicker than castor oil through a cat with diarrhoea.'

'Oh go to bed, you little pest, I've got to be up again in a few hours.'

'But will you, Cyn, will you?'

'Wait and see.'

But of course she did.

Chapter Six

'Pol? It's Bet.'

'Look, Bet, I can only spare a moment, we're on our way out — some do in the City at the Woodcutters' Hall.'

'Don't you mean Woodchoppers?'

'If you've only rung to make stupid jokes — '

'On the contrary. Unlike you, I can't afford to spend a fortune on my phone bill.'

'Well, in that case — '

'I just thought I'd let you know we've all been invited for drinks at Hopton Manor on Saturday. Cynthia Westover has issued a blanket invitation. I assume you and Pete want to come? . . . Pol, did you hear what I said?'

'Of course I heard what you said. I was just thinking it's a bit odd her ringing you, that's all. I mean, it must have been the Cornwalls who put her up to it.'

'Actually, I don't think old Monty Cornwall was involved this time . . .'

Bet had been surprised herself at the invitation from Hopton Manor, and could only assume that Simon Morris must have brought influence to bear on his cousin. Certainly the issuing of the invitation had been informal to a degree, and only three days' notice given. She'd been having a mid-morning cuppa with Christine when the phone rang. 'Mrs Brandon? Cynthia Westover here. Look, I'm frightfully sorry it's such short notice, but would you like to come for drinks on Saturday evening — six to six-thirtyish? And do bring your boy, there'll be plenty of young around.'

'That's awfully kind of you, Miss Westover. The thing is, I

do have rather a houseful, my daughter and – '

'Oh, bring the whole family, my dear, the more the merrier. Look I must dash, we've got a mare foaling. 'Bye.'

Smarting a little at the abrupt dismissal, Bet returned to her cup of tea. That was not how they issued invitations where she came from. However, Christine seemed impressed, which was something.

'Miss Cyn's really nice when you get to know her,' she said, nibbling one of Bet's chocolate digestives, 'not a bit snobbish. Of course, I've known the Manor all my life, my nan used to do the scrubbing up there when Colonel Westover, that's Miss Cyn's father, was alive, and my great-uncle George was gardener there for years. The Colonel went a bit odd in the end. He was in one of those Japanese prisoner-of-war camps and he was never the same after that, my nan said. Of course I don't remember him, really, but – '

'There's a cousin, isn't there? We met him briefly the other morning in The George.'

'Our Simon!' Inexplicably, Bet's hackles rose. If Miss Cyn, why not Mr Simon? God, this wretched place was even succeeding in making her a snob. 'Yes, Simon Morris. He was brought up at the Manor, wasn't he?'

'He's a bad boy, our Simon, but lovely with it.' To Bet's annoyance she noticed Christine was smiling reminiscently. 'He and my mum used to sit next to each other at Sunday School – little devil he was, Mum said. Miss Priddie, the Sunday School teacher, couldn't do anything with him. She complained to the Colonel in the end and they took him away. He wasn't half one for the girls, but the boys used to bully him a bit, called him The Little Wop because his dad was an Eyetie – I expect they were jealous, really.'

'Why was he brought up at the Manor?' Bet's voice was as casual as she could make it; she mustn't appear too interested. Anyway, she wasn't, was she. As it happened she needn't have bothered; Christine was already on to her. Uncle Sid Kettle had reported Simon asking leading questions on the subject of Mrs Brandon at The Waggoner the other evening. Unaware, Bet ploughed on, and managed to get a few more pertinent facts before Christine hurried off to finish polishing the mirrors in Pol's bathroom.

52

Simon's father had been an Italian restorer of antiques by the name of Angelo something-or-other. Called to the Manor to do restoration work by the old squire – Miss Cyn's grandfather – shortly before the outbreak of World War II, he had completed his task by running off with the squire's nineteen-year-old daughter, Angela, to the scandal of the surrounding neighbourhood and the fury of her parents – 'People were more straight-laced in those days, weren't they, Mrs Brandon?'

Christine was a bit vague about what happened next. All she knew was that Angelo returned to Italy soon after the outbreak of war, leaving the now pregnant Angela Westover behind in London. Whether the couple were ever actually married, she was none too sure, but as soon as the baby Simon was born, Angela's parents relented, and he was dumped down at Hopton by his mother, who promptly joined the ATS and spent the rest of the war having a whale of a time acting as driver to a succession of senior army staff-officers.

Safely cocooned in the Hopton nursery with his cousin, Cyn, Simon was happy too. And all went well until the war was over, when Angela married again – Angelo was by now safely dead; killed by an Allied bullet in North Africa in 1942 – this time a retired rubber planter, recently demobilised from the army, by the name of Reggie Morris. The couple bought a house in Camberley and set up a riding school, and for the first time in years Angela decided to take an interest in her son; he must, of course, come and live with them.

Unfortunately Simon thought otherwise. He loathed his step-father, didn't much like his mother, whom he barely knew, and kept on running back to Hopton. It didn't matter how much the Colonel leathered him on arrival; like the proverbial cat, he continued to come back. In the end everyone gave up. Angela had never been all that keen on him anyway, and had really only asked to have him back out of a belated sense of duty. Simon was sent away to boarding school, and spent his holidays at Hopton. 'So he got his own way in the end.' Christine rinsed her cup under the kitchen tap. 'But then people like him usually do, don't they.'

Predictably, the invitation to Hopton Manor was given a

pretty mixed reception by the rest of Bet's household. Nell was delighted, but immediately afterwards said she couldn't possibly go as she had nothing to wear and no time to buy anything. Diz said he thought he'd give it a miss, cocktail parties with the gentry not being much in his line. And Bernie, giving his moustache a quick comb in the kitchen mirror, said he hoped the Westover servants' hall was comfortable, because as an ex-Barton Comprehensive boy, that was where he would be entertained; at least he knew his place, if no one else did. Bet groaned and went on peeling potatoes; she knew they'd all agree to go in the end.

Later, during the washing-up, Nell said: 'Joking apart, Mum, why do you think we've been invited to the Manor? You must know how snobbish they are round here. The Rawdons — that nice couple in Buttercup Close, Bernie and I had supper with them the other night — said that unless you've lived here at least three hundred years, or you're a millionaire, people like the Westovers won't have anything to do with you socially; it isn't that they're nasty, it's just they simply don't notice you, which in a way is even worse.'

'Dear Nelly, you're such an innocent!' Diz dropped a handful of forks into the silver drawer with a crash that made his mother wince. 'Don't you realise that people from the Rectory rate higher in your actual social hierarchy than the simple denizens of a housing estate? The rector, now, would certainly come before, say, your local doctor, even possibly your local lawyer, and — '

'Two points, you berk, before I throw up,' interrupted his brother-in-law. 'One, none of us happens to be the rector; and two, the Westovers are nothing anyway, just a load of chinless idiots who happen to have inherited a house paid for by the proceeds of some sort of quack horse medicine . . .'

Quite suddenly, Bet started to giggle, and once started, couldn't stop. Shoulders shaking, eyes streaming, she hung over the sink, scrubbing ineffectively at the mashed potato saucepan in an agony of supressed laughter. 'Now look what you've done, you idiots.' Nell put a comforting hand on her mother's heaving shoulder. 'You've gone and upset Mum! She doesn't have much of a life down here, and all you two can do when she is asked out, is try and spoil it for her.'

54

'She's not crying, she's laughing.' Diz knew his mother better than the others. Nell went pink. 'Quite honestly, Mum, I can't see it's that funny.'

'Oh darling, it isn't, not really, — you're quite right. It's just ... well, it was the cousin, you see. I happened to meet him in the wood — I must have forgotten to tell you. He ... he was quite friendly, actually, in spite of the dogs, and I think it may be because of him we've been asked.'

Suddenly everyone shut up. What was so funny about meeting the cousin? Which cousin, anyway? Diz glanced sharply at his mother, remembering Mr Bone. He hoped she wasn't getting peculiar.

It was more or less dark by the time they set out for Hopton Manor the following Saturday. Bet was right, everyone had agreed to go in the end. Admittedly, she'd had a bit of a struggle with Diz over his party outfit, in the course of which he'd threatened once again not to attend. He'd appeared downstairs in jeans and an army surplus shirt, and it was only after repeated threats from her and much cajolery from his sister that he was finally won over and agreed to change into his only suit; last worn, he reminded them bitterly, at his father's funeral.

Nell had been reduced to tears over her outfit. At considerable expense and after much soul-searching, she'd gone mad and purchased herself a jade-green two piece of a somewhat way-out design, only to be told at the last minute by Bernie that it made her look like someone in a pantomime. Tearfully refusing ever to be seen in the outfit again, she ended up wearing a rather sexy cocktail frock borrowed from Pol. Pol herself naturally looked exactly right in a soft tweed dress which must have cost the earth, and a pearl choker.

As a result of all this Bet was left with little time to spend on her own appearance. Too late, she noticed a soup mark on her red dress, and her mascara brush had somehow gone all gooey, causing her eyelashes to stick together. But it couldn't be helped, and after one last, despairing look in her rather murky bedroom mirror — the others having commandeered the one in the bathroom — she hurried downstairs to join the Redfords.

'Bet, did you know you've smudged your mascara? You should have done your face in my bathroom, that bedroom of yours is a positive black hole. I can't imagine why – '

'Oh shut up, Pol. Who's going to look at me anyway?'

As the crow flies, Hopton Manor, set in a shallow valley on the far side of the wood, was only a mile from the Rectory; however, by road it was nearly three. The drive gates were imposing enough, their effect slightly marred by the fact that they were propped open with an aluminium dustbin. The drive itself was full of potholes and seemed to go on for miles. The house, when they reached it at last, a crouching mass in the gathering dark, looked vaguely Queen Anne. However, as no welcoming light shone from its elegantly proportioned windows – not even a cheery gleam from a lantern in the porch – it was hard to make out what it was like. In point of fact the whole place looked utterly dead. Had they come on the wrong night? Somewhere quite near an owl hooted, and from the woods behind the house came the harsh, mournful bark of a mating fox.

Trespassers, they tiptoed across the gravel to the front door, the sound of their feet on the stones painfully loud in the all-enveloping silence, and huddled in the porch while Diz boldly grasped the ancient doorknocker – there didn't seem to be a bell – and gave several loud raps on the front door.

Nothing happened.

'Bet, are you sure you've got the date right?' Pol hugged her fur coat. 'Of course I've got the date right. Miss Westover definitely said Saturday.'

Actually, Bet was beginning to have doubts about this. 'Give the knocker another go, Diz,' she hissed, 'someone must be there.' Diz obediently did as he was told. 'Is anybody there?' he shouted into the unresponsive darkness. At that moment the door opened and he was propelled abruptly into a vast, cluttered hall, lit, it appeared, by a single forty-watt bulb.

'Good evenings?' A tall, extremely handsome manservant encased in tight, perfectly cut black trousers and a dazzling white jacket stood before them, the expression on his face one of chilling disapproval. 'Mrs Brandon and party from the Rectory – WE HAVE BEEN INVITED,' Pete shouted in his best talking-to-foreigners voice. 'Si si.' The manservant nodded impatiently and waved them in the direction of a door to the right of the staircase, then promptly disappeared into the surrounding gloom. Nell nudged her mother. 'Let's hope there are more like him around, eh, Mum!' Bernie's face, already grim, took on an even grimmer aspect. Far away, at the end of a long passage, in another world of warmth and light and laughter, Bet thought she heard the sounds of a party.

The room into which they'd been ushered so unceremoniously turned out to be a cloakroom cluttered with damp mackintoshes, wellies, old walking sticks and fishing gear; it was freezing cold, and smelt strongly of cat. Too cold to take their coats off, they stood around glumly waiting for something to happen.

At last — just as Diz, bored with hanging about, had taken down a fishing rod, placed an aged deerstalker on his head and, despite protests from Bet, was about to launch into one of his impersonations — there came a shriek from the doorway. 'My poor dears! That adorable Alfonso has shown you into the gents! I really am most frightfully sorry. My name's Sonia Byngham-Smythe, by the way, and you simply must be the party from the Rectory.'

They nodded, even Pol bereft of words. Mrs. Byngham-Smythe was indeed an apparition. Clad in green lurex tights topped by a tunic of purple silk, her age impossible to determine, she looked Bet up and down, her enormous, mascara-caked eyes taking in every detail of her appearance. 'And you *must* be Mrs. Brandon.' Bet placed her hand defensively over the soup stain. 'Is that enchanting boy your son? How lucky you are — I've only a dismal daughter.'

'Introductions are in order, I think.' Pol moved gracefully forward, it was time to take over. 'I'm Polly Redford, this is my husband, Peter, my niece Nell Sparsworth and her husband, Bernard. The boy in the hat is my nephew, Desmond. It's too awful that there are so many of us, but I gather from my sister that Miss Westover did very kindly issue a blanket invitation. The traumas one has to endure with one's Spanish staff! So decorative, but their English does sometimes leave something to be desired.'

Mrs. Byngham-Smythe looked at Pol thoughtfully, acknowledging a worthy opponent, and Bet swelled with pride for her sister. They were ushered upstairs without further ado, leaving Pete, Bernie and Diz to wait for them in the hall.

The ladies' cloaks turned out to be a large, gloomy bedroom hung about with depressing prints of a quasi-religious nature and lit again, it seemed, by a forty-watt bulb. 'Come down, darlings, when you're ready, Alfonso will show you the way,' shrieked Mrs Byngham-Smythe with a frightening smile. Her perfume remained behind her, the fumes so powerful they made Bet's eyes water. She turned to her sister — always give praise where praise is due — 'Pol you were marvellous, you really were.' Pol smiled happily; Bet so seldom approved of anything one did. 'I do occasionally have my uses ...'

'Whoever can that woman be, Aunt Pol. Is she some sort of relative?' Pol smoothed her beautifully cut dress over her hips; she didn't have to look in the mirror, she knew her make-up was perfect. 'She's another cousin, the Hon. Mrs Byngham-Smythe, one reads of her occasionally in the gossip columns. She's been married umpteen times, drinks like a fish and will sleep with virtually anything, including the dog if pushed, or so I've heard.' Bet and her daughter looked at one another in awe; they did not know these things.

Out on the landing, they peered into the gloom of the hall below; inevitably, there was no sign of Alfonso. Instead they were met with the sight of Diz lying on his stomach, apparently trying to retrieve something from under a rather dusty, rather beautiful, carved oak chest. Crouched beside him, Bernie looked resigned and Pete harassed. 'He's only broken a knob off this chest!' said Bernie in his I-told-you-something-like-this-would-happen voice. 'He said it was fake and gave it a tug and it flew off and rolled under there.'

'For heaven's sake, Pete, are you incapable of keeping a seventeen-year-old boy under control for two minutes?' Pol's question was purely rhetorical and Pete decided to ignore it. 'Ah, there you are at last. Come on, Diz, forget about that damned knob and let's find the party, it looks as if Alfonso's disappeared for good.'

'Probably eloped with our Sonia.' Diz emerged, covered in dust. Bet made a few ineffectual attempts to tidy him up, but he brushed her hand away, and the party set off in Indian file down the long passage leading out of the hall, at the end of which was to be heard a noise like the distant baying of hounds. 'The drinking call of the upper classes at the water-hole,' Bernie hissed at Nell as they hurried down the passage, stumbling now and again in the inky darkness.

Emerging at last into the light, they found themselves in a huge, brilliantly lit room, stiflingly hot and already packed with people. Cynthia Westover was standing just inside the door, looking more than ever like the school hockey captain in mufti. Her blonde-streaked hair was permed tightly in the style of the nineteen forties, and she wore a plain shirt-waister of a rather unpleasant shade of puce. 'Ah, Mrs Brandon. You've found your way at last! I'm sure there are plenty of people you know. Do grab yourselves a drink — the bar's over there.' She pointed vaguely towards the far end of the room. Not a sign of Simon Morris anywhere.

The bar, when they finally reached it, turned out to be a long table loaded with food and drink of every description. Whatever Ms Westover saved on electricity, she undoubtedly spent on alcohol. It was presided over by Alfonso and a spotty girl from the village who Bet was pretty sure was yet another member of the ubiquitous Kettle clan.

'This is more like it!' Diz gulped down a champagne cocktail before Bet could stop him. 'It's only for the cherry, Mum, don't panic.' Bet shrugged and looked about her; she hadn't come here to play the heavy parent, she'd come to . . . Oh, hell, she surely wasn't going to be so childish as to feel disappointed. But if Simon wasn't going to be there, why had he asked her? But perhaps he wasn't the one who had asked her; of course, that was an idea she'd dreamed up out of her imagination. And what did it matter anyway. Feeling like an Eskimo suddenly dumped down in the middle of an Arab market, she peered dismally up at the rather bad portrait of Saltpeter Westover above the mantlepiece and waited for something to happen.

'Peter, my dear chap, how are you? We hoped we might bump into you here.'

'Monty! Just the man I want to see.'

A tall man with a receding chin, who looked like a nineteenth-century cavalry officer in a Victorian print, had suddenly emerged from the crowd. Old Monty Cornwall at last! Behind him was his wife, Kitty, a replica of him except that she wore glasses. Pol kissed her fondly. 'My dear, I feel absolutely awful I haven't rung, but we've been inundated with builders and – '

'My dear, so have we. I do so sympathise. Now do introduce us, we've been dying to meet your sister.' There were shouted introductions all round, and the Rectory party gave a brief account of the rigors of their arrival. 'Oh you poor dears! Cyn Westover has a heart of gold, but no manners whatever, none of the family has. Desmond, you simply must meet my daughter, she's going up to Oxford in October so you're sure to have something in common.' Diz looked doubtful, but allowed himself to be led away in the direction of a group of noisy teenagers in the far corner of the room. They were all, Bet noticed, wearing jeans; there would, she supposed gloomily, be recriminations later on.

'Come and meet the Campbells.' Monty Cornwall made an all-embracing gesture. 'They must be about your nearest neighbours. Frightfully nice couple – retired now, of course. I believe he used to run the gasworks in Bogota. They're over there under the window, talking to the woman with a feather in her hat.' Pol, Pete and the Sparsworths set off obediently behind him as he hoved his way through the crowd, despite the fact that the Campbells and their connection with the gas works in Bogota did not, on the face of it, sound all that exciting. Anything, Nell whispered to Bernie, was better than standing at the bar like a bunch of wallflowers. Bet, feeling rebellious, remained where she was and ordered another champagne cocktail.

'You live in the Old Rectory at Hopton, don't you?' A timid voice sounded in her ear, reminding her forcefully of the caterpillar in *Alice in Wonderland*. 'Yes we do,' she said, smiling brightly. A sad, lost little lady stood beside her, dressed in what looked like one of those mail-order dresses advertised in Sunday newspapers, whose style never seems to change. They talked in a desultory fashion. The lady turned out to be the local librarian; she was pretty sure, she confided to Bet, that she had been invited by mistake. She had a feeling, she said, that Miss Westover had somehow got her lists mixed up. 'Not that I mind, Mrs Brandon, don't get me wrong,' she gave a shrill laugh, the gin in her bitter lemon beginning to take effect, 'if it gives me a chance to see inside this lovely old place.' And so it went on. Bet was passed from group to group, each time reciting her credentials until she began to wish she'd had them typed out beforehand, a sort of social CV to be handed out to interested parties on request.

What seemed hours later, she found herself standing in a corner with another tiny lady − only this one had her hair cut in an Eton crop − holding a rather one-sided conversation on the subject of the Saxon village at West Stowe. Bet knew little, actually nothing, about West Stowe, and simply stood there, sipping her drink and trying to look intelligent. She hadn't seen the rest of her lot since they'd departed in search of the people from Bogota. 'You see, Mrs Brandon, what I feel about all this so-called reconstruction is −'

'Hullo, Titania, how goes it?'

Bet spun round, spilling most of her drink in the process. Simon Morris, looking not cross this time but tired, smiled at her. 'Hullo there, Smoky,' said the West Stowe lady unexpectedly, 'so you know Mrs Brandon.'

'We've met here and there. And how are you, Tabby? Still mating all those gorgeous red setters and enjoying every minute of it?'

'You really are the wickedest man! Of course I don't enjoy it!' The West Stowe lady positively glowed, the ethics of pseudo-historical reconstruction forgotten. A horsey woman with an eye-glass loomed up. 'Tabby, my dear, I want to pick your brains about Golden Joseph − what price Crufts now, eh?'

'Why Titania?'

'We met in a wood, didn't we.'

'But if I'm Titania, who . . .?'

'Bottom probably. I sometimes think an ass's head would suit me admirably.'

'I can't think where my family have got to.' Bet, far out of her depths, felt herself being swept along by currents she

61

never new existed. 'I don't seem to have seen them for hours.'

'Have dinner with me?'

'I'd like to ... When you're next down, perhaps, and you must come and –'

'I meant now, actually. My car broke down on the A12 on the way here, I had the father and mother of a row with my director this morning, and what with one thing and another I don't think I can take much more of this mob, God knows where Cyn digs them up. Will you?'

Quite suddenly, absurdly, she felt relieved; he had, after all, come as quickly as he could. To hell with the family, why shouldn't she have dinner with Simon? 'I'd like to,' she said, feeling both reckless and wicked (why did she feel wicked?), 'but I must tell the others.'

'We can tell Cyn on the way out, don't worry. Surely they're capable of looking after themselves?'

'Ah, there you are at last, Bet. We were wondering where you'd got to. How's the car, Morris, no problems, I hope?' Pete was showing signs of wear – a statue of Bacchus a bit blurred round the edges from being left too long in the rain. 'Pete, I'm so glad you've appeared, I was just going to look for you. Mr Morris has very kindly asked me to dinner, so I won't be home until later on.'

'Splendid, splendid!' Actually Pete looked none too pleased, his pale blue, somewhat bloodshot eyes darting suspiciously from Simon to Bet and back again to Simon. He helped himself to a passing drink and tried again. 'Look, I've just had an idea. We're all going on somewhere with the Cornwalls; why not join forces?'

'Sorry, Redford, but count me out. I've had a pig of a day, added to which I was up most of last night with a bunch of fellow hacks at a Press do, and quite frankly I don't think I could cope with a large party. Your sister-in-law here has kindly agreed to take pity on me and keep me company over a quiet meal at The George, after which I hope to have an early night.' Pete closed his eyes, then opened them again and took a pull at his drink. Damned cheek! 'Well I suppose if Bet would rather –'

'I would rather – really I would. You know I don't like big

62

parties.' (Did he?) 'And I'll be home hours before the rest of you.'

'If that's what you want ... It seems a shame, the Cornwalls are dying to meet you properly, Kitty was only saying — '

'Look, Redford, we must dash, otherwise we'll never get a table. Come along, Mrs B., where did you leave your coat ...?'

'Remember not to blame me when it all goes wrong,' Cyn Westover shouted after Simon as he and Bet made for the door. Outside in the passage the cold hit them; it was like being enveloped in an icy blanket. 'What did your cousin mean about it all going wrong?'

'Look, you can nip up the back stairs to collect your coat; turn right at the top and then second left, you can't miss it. I'll wait for you here, but hurry or we really won't get a table.'

It was freezing hard now outside. Bright moonlight on the red damask curtains in the ladies' cloaks turned it into a bedroom from *Jane Eyre*. Was there a poor, demented Mrs Rochester hidden somewhere in the attics? Bet hurried into her coat, teeth chattering, glanced briefly at the over-made-up stranger in the Victorian mahogany pier-glass, and went in search of Simon.

'I think we'd better take Cyn's Lancia,' he said as they emerged into a large courtyard packed with cars, at the back of the house. 'My old heap's behaving a bit oddly, it hasn't recovered yet from Sid Kettle's service.' Hands in the pockets of his sheepskin coat, he set off at speed across the yard, Bet tottering behind him, her high heels slipping on the frozen cobbles. 'I see now where we went wrong,' she shouted, trying to catch up, 'we used the front drive. No wonder everything was so quiet — we thought we'd come on the wrong night.'

'Good Lord, did you really? We don't use the front drive, haven't done for years. Didn't Cyn tell you? No doubt your esteemed brother-in-law was driving?'

'No, she didn't tell us, and yes, he was, although I don't see what that's got to do with it. We do happen to be new in the neighbourhood, in case you've forgotten, and oddly enough the question of whether the Westovers use their front drive or simply slum it in the back doesn't happen to have been on our list of priorities.'

At least that made him take notice. He gave a bark of laughter and looked round. 'She bites, then, does she? I knew she would. I'm sorry, one's arrogance is quite appalling; whether or not we use our front drive is indeed of no interest to anyone. I was just worried about the springs on your brother-in-law's car, that's all.'

'Balls!' But she took his hand all the same.

Nell Gwynne's Buttery at The George turned out to be practically empty when they got there. Music of an unidentifiable nature treacled out of the walls, the latter liberally sprinkled with oranges and a mural in which a cloaked figure in a broad-brimmed hat played a guitar to a lady with large bosoms, who hung perilously out of the upper window of a cardboard-looking tower. The air was redolent of fried onions and lunchtime curry. They chose a table as far away from the kitchens as possible and sat down.

Simon looked about him. 'I remember this place when it was all stained white tablecloths, brown Windsor soup, and big fat ladies in pudding-basin hats tucking into toad-in-the-hole and spotted dick and custard. There used to be two stuffed otters and a water rat in a glass case over there by the window; I'd spend hours looking at those otters when I was a lad. On market days the place was so packed you had to queue. There was a waitress here then called Dawn, with mean eyes and red hair, whom I used to dream about all through the school term. When I came back one holidays, she'd upped and joined the WAAF; it broke my heart. I met her again some years later and she'd turned into a large lady in a pudding-basin hat. Life is sad, Bet Brandon, is it not?' Bet nodded dreamily. She was beginning to feel like someone in a film – Lauren Bacall, perhaps. Simon was a bit drunk of course, but then so was she . . .

'Hullo, stranger! We don't often see you here these days. How are they at the Manor – Miss Cyn keeping well?' The waitress, yet another large lady, but in place of the pudding-basin hat, blue plastic earrings in the shape of miniature elephants and hair like a cone of pink ice-cream. Did Simon know everyone? Bet wondered idly what it would be like to be part of a family who'd lived in the same place for four hundred years.

'What's it to be, then?' Simon said. 'Frozen scampi with a blob of Thelma's own special mayonnaise, or the duck à l'orange? I'm chancing my arm with prawn cocktail and the scampi.'

'I'll have the same,' she said, not caring really.

'Two of both, then, Thelm, and make sure the chips are thawed out, won't you, I don't want to be up all night.' Thelma gave a shriek that rattled the glasses on the empty tables; 'You don't change, do you, Simmy!' She turned to Bet. 'He used to be a real little devil. I could tell you a few tales. If you want to know what a monkey he is, you ask him about Miss Priddie's bible class ...' More cackles. Simon seemed quite unmoved by the banter, indeed enjoying it, but behind it all Bet noticed that Thelma's eyes were shrewd and appraising — Our Sim's got a new lady friend, she'd report later to anyone interested, I wonder how long she'll last?

When she'd gone ('Chef'll have my guts for garters if I don't hurry up with the orders, he wants to be off home in time for "Match of the Day"'.) Simon said: 'You're very quiet. Sorry you came?'

'No,' Bet said, trying to work out the exact colour of his eyes; most of the time they were a sort of chestnut brown, but sometimes much paler than that and sometimes almost black. 'I was thinking, that's all.'

'Poor Bet, is it very lonely?' Simon reached out his hand across the table.

'No, no of course it isn't, I'm far too busy to be lonely.' But she took the hand, all the same — chewed nails, she noticed, gold signet ring on the little finger. Then suddenly, not knowing why, she gave in. 'Sometimes it's hell, actually,' she said, 'but then one always assumed it would be.' (Shouldn't she take her hand away — could she take her hand away?)

'Will I make you better?'

She wished she didn't feel so faint, could think more clearly. His voice was the voice of a tempter, but then almost all of her wanted to be tempted; there was this tiny bit that didn't, and it would probably be bigger by morning, but tonight ... She swallowed, aware now only of the chemistry between them.

'Two prawn cocktails coming up and what about some

vino?' Thelma, with a jangle of earrings, plonked a bilious pink mixture in front of her, and Bet, feeling like the lonely prawn adhering to the rim of the glass dish in which the mixture came, snatched her hand away from Simon's and took a bread roll instead. For a second Simon, whose expression up to now had been that of a rather vulnerable small boy unpacking his first Christmas present, appeared nonplussed, but only for a second. Even before Bet had bitten into her unwanted roll, he'd turned back into the world-weary, slightly saturnine Simon she knew. And by the time Thelma, with a final wiggle of the hips and a shriek like a macaw, had departed for the kitchen, life had returned to normal.

Simon dug a spoon into his prawn cocktail. 'To take away the taste of this,' he said, putting the spoon down again and grinning across the table at her, 'I could, if you like, tell you about old Saltpeter Westover. He was quite an amusing cove actually – about the only Westover who was – and although I says it myself, I'm not a bad hand at telling a story. Or if you prefer something lighter, what about my experiences as a courier in the travel business? The time I lost a party of Ulster Protestants bound for the Costa del Sol at Gatwick and they caught the wrong plane and landed up in Lourdes?'

And Bet, opting for the travel business, listened and laughed until she cried. For Simon Morris could be both funny and charming when he tried, and tonight he was trying his very hardest.

It was past midnight when they left the restaurant. Outside, in the market square, motor-cycles snarled and spiky-haired young erupted from Dirty Dan's Disco on the corner by the Methodist church. 'Did you know,' Simon said, weaving Cyn's Lancia in and out of the motor-cycles, 'that a Protestant martyr was burned in this square in 1556? A kind old buffer, people said, greatly skilled in the art of healing. That didn't save him, however, though they did put green wood on the fire to hasten his end.'

'Green wood?'

'You're asphyxiated by the smoke before the fire gets you.'

'Oh.'

They didn't talk much after that until Simon stopped the

car at the Rectory gate. 'I won't drive in, Titania, I've no desire to rouse your family, and it looks as though they're back. It's been a great evening, and thank you for putting up with me.'

So he wasn't going to try and kiss her. Would she have let him if he had? No need to answer that one, not now anyway. He opened the car door and she scrambled out and stood on the grass verge, looking in through the window. 'I've enjoyed it, too, even the chips and the history.'

'Am I a bore about history?' Now he was looking vulnerable again, and Bet was a sucker for vulnerability. 'No, you're not a bore about history,' she said, 'you're not a bore about anything — goodnight.'

'Goodnight, Titania . . . and don't let that family of yours bully you.' She watched him turn the big car in the narrow lane and went on standing there on the frosty grass until the sound of its engine had died away, then turned and went into the house. Warm, humming darkness enveloped her. She switched on the light and Tib raised a sleepy head in greeting, then sank back into his basket. Thank God, the others must have gone to bed.

'Pete,' Pol poked her husband in the ribs, 'I think I heard a car. Go and have a look out of the landing window.'

'For God's sake, ducky, it's none of our business when Bet gets home.'

'You've simply no feeling for anyone else, have you. Bet could have been raped, or anything. You know what the Normans said about that man and his reputation.' Pete, however, was asleep again, there would be no further assistance from him; the house could burn down for all he cared! She supposed she'd have to go and see for herself — someone had to.

Throwing a dressing-gown round her shoulders Pol hurried out on to the landing and twitched back the curtain. It was dark outside, the moon eclipsed by scurrying clouds, but through the darkness, light from Bet's kitchen streamed out across the yard — she was home. Thank God for that! No sound of voices, either, so she couldn't have asked him in; one must be grateful for small mercies.

Pete was snoring when she got back into bed. It was no good, if he was going to make that sort of noise she'd have to take a sleeping pill . . .

Nell also heard the car. She'd like to have woken Bernie to tell him, but unfortunately they weren't on speaking terms. There had been a slight incident earlier in the evening when, with some abandon, she'd kicked off her shoes and danced with a young man Bernie had described later as a half-witted Hooray Henry, and she'd not unnaturally taken exception. Anyway, what was wrong with being a Hooray Henry – at least this one had nice manners and could dance, which was more than you could say for Bernie . . .

Diz heard nothing. He lay on his back, dead to the world, a bowl placed strategically beside his bed, the alcoholic excesses of his evening forgotten in insensibility.

Chapter Seven

'Stand clear of the gates,' the familiar robot voice intoned as the lift at Hampstead tube station began its slow, creaking journey to the surface with Bet the only passenger. She felt a little self-conscious, and was glad to escape at the top into the roar of the traffic grinding up Heath Street. It was a bright, windy day nearly two weeks after the Westover party and Bet was on her way to visit Miles's grave.

Not that he would have approved, he'd always wanted to be cremated. But when the time came she'd pleaded with him to change his mind, unable to bear the thought of his body being hygienically reduced to ashes, and too weak for further argument, he'd given in. Anyway, he'd said, smiling a little at the feeble joke, it would be nice to have Hugh Gaitskell as a neighbour, at least they'd been on the same side.

Turning up Church Street, a gust of wind caught her hair, blowing it across her face so that for a moment she couldn't see. She shivered, tightly clutching the carefully wrapped spring flowers she had picked from the garden that morning before catching the train. 'Buy some lucky heather, dearie?' the gypsy woman at the cemetery gates called after her, 'you have a lucky face.' She'd said the same thing, Bet remembered, on the day of Miles's funeral.

His grave, when she found it, looked just like any other; the headstone was a bit newer, that was all. *Miles Desmond Brandon, beloved husband of* . . . But of course Miles wasn't there, was he, he never had been. Feeling self-conscious again, she knelt down on the damp grass, and placing her flowers neatly beside the headstone, closed her eyes. But it was no good, all she could think of was that she was kneeling on something sharp, and that when she got up her skirt would have a damp stain on the front. She shifted uncomfortably and suddenly, inside her head, heard Miles' voice – the one he used when he was laughing at her. 'Darling, you're such an ass sometimes – no need for all this . . .' She opened her eyes and found a large, hairy, surprised-looking dog squatting on his haunches beside her. 'Roddy, come here at once!' A woman's voice, sharp with embarrassment. 'Don't be such a bloody nuisance.' The dog took one more look at Bet, then bounded away. He was a young dog, joyous, full of life and curiosity. Bet stood up, smiling foolishly to herself, and brushed the grass from her skirt, then turned, and picking her way carefully through the forest of white headstones, slowly retraced her steps to the cemetery gates.

There was nothing for her here.

She didn't after all go and have a nostalgic look at the house in Thorn Lane; she'd planned to, but somehow now there seemed no point. In a few short months she had become a stranger in a part of London once so utterly familiar that to return to it after an absence was like putting on an old and valued coat, a coat in which every tear in the lining, every hanging thread, every stain, held some sort of memory. Now the coat had gone to the jumble sale and the new one didn't fit.

Instead she had coffee in a new place on Haverstock Hill, and shocked herself by thinking about Simon Morris. Had Simon been what this trip was all about? A cack-handed attempt at getting rid of her guilt about wanting someone other than Miles? She bit sadly into her too-large Danish pastry – she hadn't been able to resist it and now didn't want it – and admitted that it probably was. No wonder Miles had laughed at her, he had every right to, she was behaving like the heroine in a nineteenth-century melodrama.

She took another sip of coffee and wondered for the umpteenth time what had happened to Simon since the night of the party and why he had so obstinately refused to get in touch. Busy, she'd repeatedly told herself, busy; but by now the excuse was wearing thin, and to be honest, he didn't seem the type to put business before pleasure. Perhaps taking her out to dinner hadn't been a pleasure? Of course the trouble was, she was quite unused to situations of this sort, it was a very long time since she'd been in one. Certainly, in those dim, distant days before Miles, if someone took her out and looked at her in the way Simon had looked at her, he always made damned sure he tried to take her out again; the only question being whether or not she herself liked him sufficiently to wish to repeat the experience. What a spoilt little bitch she must have been!

To be fair, though, what she was suffering from now wasn't so much hurt pride because Simon had not found her sufficiently interesting or attractive (it must be said) to press his suit, it was much more a kind of bitter disappointment. The thing was, she'd never encountered anyone quite like Simon before. There was something about that mixture of upper-crust savoir-faire, hopelessness, and the ability to make her laugh until she cried, that she seemd to find totally irresistible. The rather lowering fact that, no temptation having been offered, there was nothing for her to resist, served only to make the whole business more intriguing. And it wasn't as if her family had helped much, either.

Her family were another reason why Bet had come to London; she had felt she simply had to escape from them, if only for a day. Ever since the Westover party, the atmosphere at the Rectory had simply not been right. Things started to go wrong, in fact, the very morning after the party. Fair enough, everyone, with the exception of Pol and herself, was recovering from a serious hangover. But the trouble was, they had continued to go wrong ever since. Was this the evil power of alcohol, or had they all been bewitched by the Westovers? And yet despite all this, and despite her own bitter disappointment at the subsequent non-appearance of Simon, she felt more alive than she had in years. Perhaps, who knew, this was the root of the trouble?

Bet had woken that Sunday morning after the party with no trace of a hangover, just the expectation of fun to come, like a child on its birthday morning. Bouncing downstairs to get breakfast, she had arrived in the kitchen to be confronted by the pale, sickly and reproachful faces of her son and daughter.

71

'Hullo, darlings, had a good evening? Bernie still in bed?'

'Bernie's gone to spend the day with his parents,' Nell said repressively, 'he thought it was time he paid them a visit.'

'But why didn't you go, darling, it's such a lovely day – '

'We don't have to do everything together, for goodness sake. Anyway, his mother will be delighted, she prefers to have her darling boy on his own, as well you know, Mum.'

Unable to think of a suitable reply to this – it was true, but to admit it was true would surely be a mistake, and in any case Nell, clutching a mug of black coffee to her bosom, had already flounced out of the room – Bet turned her attention to her son. What, she asked brightly, did he fancy for his breakfast? Nothing, he said, sipping a fizzing glass of alka seltzer and not looking at her. The last thing he wanted was food, he should have thought that would have been obvious to anyone. He'd only come down to get a drink and was on his way back to bed. Still too pre-occupied with her own thoughts to read the storm cones in the atmosphere, Bet asked him how he'd fared the previous evening. He closed his eyes. He couldn't remember, he said, it wasn't that important anyway, but he was fairly sure that Mrs Byngham-Smythe had made a pass at him. 'But darling, she *can't* have done! I mean, she must be old enough to be your grandmother – '

'You wouldn't know, would you. You were too busy getting yourself picked up to have time to think about anyone else.'

'Diz! I will not let you speak to me like that. Just because your father isn't here, there's no need to think you can behave as you like – '

'Well, if he had been he'd soon have given that Morris guy a punch up the arsehole.'

'How dare you!' Bet, seizing the fish-slice, prepared for battle. But Diz had already fled, and by the noise emanating from the downstairs loo, was being sick again.

Then there had been the Redfords.

Peter had bearded her in the garden later on that morning. There had been little point in preparing Sunday lunch with no one to eat it. 'Ah, here you are, ducky,' and she'd known at once by the sound of his voice that he'd been sent by Pol to do a bit of fishing.

'Yes, here I am, Pete, whole and in one piece. And how are you? Feeling a tiny bit under the weather, are we?' Pete waved an arm about as though swatting an imaginary fly, and stepped heavily on the lupin she'd just that moment planted. 'Pete, get *off*! Can't you see you're standing on the garden —'

'Never mind the garden, ducky —'

'What d'you mean, never mind the garden? Don't you want me to get on with the garden, then? I've no doubt you and Pol will be the first to take advantage of it when you bring your posh friends down in the summer.'

Pete put a hand on her shoulder. 'Calm down, ducky, for goodness sake. I've only come to ask if you felt strong enough to pop in for a noggin around twelve-thirty, that's all.'

'Of course I feel strong enough — why on earth shouldn't I?' Bet said. At that precise moment the phone rang, making her stomach lurch. Simon? 'Look that's our phone, Pete, I'd better answer it, no one else is about.'

The phone, as if to defy her, promptly stopped ringing. 'A bit on the *qui vive* aren't we? Waiting for a call from the boyfriend? Apologising for keeping you out so late, no doubt. What time did you get in, by the way? I thought the chap said he wanted an early night.'

Bet swallowed; the call must have been for Nell. Why didn't everyone leave her alone? 'Oh go away, Pete, can't you see I'm busy?'

'OK, OK, I know when I'm not wanted —'

'You could have fooled me.'

'Now, now, pussy cat,' Pete bent down and kissed the back of her neck as she crouched crossly at his feet, trowel in hand, 'no need to show your claws; keep them for Mr Morris —'

'Pete!' But he'd dodged away before she could get at him, this time flattening the pale green shoots of a young delphinium which, as a result of the vast quantities of loving care, and slug death, expended upon it, had been just on the verge of maturity.

Having decided not to accept the Redfords' invitation for drinks, Bet accepted it. Of course to do so would be a mistake, she'd known this, but all the same she went. Disapproval still prevailed in her part of the house, and after that first time, the phone had obstinately refused to ring.

Since it was such a lovely day they had their drinks on the verandah. At first everything went surprisingly smoothly and Bet felt herself beginning to relax as she lounged in her bright patio chair, sleepily sipping an ice-cold gin and cin − Pol did these things so well − and watching an early bee crawl industriously in and out of the fat, smoke-blue wisteria buds that dangled from the newly-painted wrought-ironwork above her head.

Then Pol had to go and spoil it all. 'Now, Bet,' she said, smiling in a way that had infuriated Bet for as long as she could remember, 'it really was a good dinner last night, wasn't it, Pete? Such a pity you and your new friend didn't come, I'm sure you would have enjoyed it. The Cornwalls say that the Mulberry Bush is by far the best place to eat round here.'

Here we go! Bet took a deep breath and prepared for battle. 'Well, of course, if the Cornwalls say so, it must be! Anyway, as he told Pete, my so-called 'new friend' was more or less dead on his feet. He'd been up most of the previous night at some press do, and the last thing he wanted was to −'

'Launching a new deodorant for dogs, so I heard. The chap does work for Smike McGregor, doesn't he?'

'He's in advertising, yes. I can't see that it matters which particular firm − I know he's one of their top copywriters.'

'Told you so, did he?' Pete had not forgotten the look of bored contempt that Simon had treated him to. 'I should think it does matter, though, ducky, because the buzz is that Smike McGregor are on their way out. Oddly enough, old Dicky Dashwood was only talking about them the other day. It seems that −'

'Oh shut up, Pete, I'm sure Bet has no desire to listen to City gossip and I'm quite sure I haven't. Nor is there the slightest need for Bet to jump so valiantly to the defence of her hero. The Cornwalls quite understood. It was palpably obvious to anyone that the man wanted to get her away from us, and knowing Bet's predilection for Italian males as I do, I'm not in the least surprised he succeeded. I'll never forget the fuss she kicked up about that awful barman in Capri, Mum and Dad practically had to lock her in her bedroom, she −'

'If you must bandy insults,' Bet was getting angry now, 'you might at least have the guts to address them to me instead of going on as if I wasn't here.'

'Steady on, girls, no need to get your knickers in a twist!'

'Please don't interfere, Pete, and you don't have to get vulgar either.' Pol held out her glass for a refill.

'Sorry, I'm sure. I was only trying to – '

'Pete!'

'Oh, all right then.' Pete refilled his wife's glass and passed a dish of salted almonds to his smouldering sister-in-law. 'But joking apart, Bet,' (joking?) 'there is just one small point. If the chap was as fagged out as he said he was, how come he didn't bring you home until gone midnight?'

'And how, may one ask, do you know what time he brought me home? You were all in bed.' Pete cast an agonised eye at his wife. 'Well, actually ...'

'Because the car made such a noise it woke me up.' Pol, also getting angry, leaped to his rescue. 'And then of course I couldn't get to sleep again and had to take a sleeping pill. But surely, Bet, even you aren't going to blame us for being worried! I should have thought you'd be pleased that somebody cared enough about you to worry when you disappear into the night with a complete stranger.'

'Aren't I a bit old to be raped?'

'Age doesn't come into it. There was an old lady of eighty only last week – chap of sixteen ...' Pol closed her eyes. 'Just pop into the kitchen, Pete, and take the lemon sorbet out of the freezer, it'll need thawing out.'

'But surely – '

'Pete, please do as I say.' Pete went, and Pol, beginning to think she'd gone too far, decided to backtrack. 'He means well, but sometimes ... well, you know.' She smiled placatingly.

Bet, however, was in no mood for olive branches. She stood up and carefully placed her empty glass on the patio table. 'Look, Pol, I would like to make one thing quite clear, then I swear I won't mention the subject again – that is, if you don't. The fact that we all live under the same roof does not in any way whatever give you the right to interfere in my life. If I meet someone and become friendly with him, that's my business; if we sleep together, that's also my business – '

'Oh God, you haven't, Bet! Not yet, surely – Kitty Cornwall said – '

'How dare you discuss me with Kitty Cornwall! What I choose to do or not to do is entirely my own affair. Do I make myself clear?'

By this time Pol was standing too. She was also trembling a little; like most people who spend much of their time being rude to others, she was shattered when the compliment was returned. 'I'm sorry if I've offended you, Bet. I – that is, Pete and I – only meant it for the best. After all it's not much more than a year since Miles's death, and for you to become entangled with someone of Simon Morris's reputation – Kitty Cornwall told us . . .'

But Bet had gone, slamming the sitting-room door so hard that one of Pol's precious Spode plates fell off the mantle-piece and would have shattered in a thousand bits if, as she told Pete afterwards, she hadn't been there to catch it. Since then they hadn't spoken; Bet hadn't even rung Pol about coming to London . . .

Bet looked at her watch. Not yet twelve, but she was fed up with sitting in the café staring at the oddities wandering up and down Haverstock Hill, and the noise of the traffic was giving her a headache. She got up from the table and wandered over to the counter to pay for her coffee. The waitress accepted her money, scarcely bothering to raise her eyes from the magazine she was reading.

Outside the sun shone, but the cold wind blew dust in her eyes and made her shiver. Somehow, now, it all seemed rather absurd, Pol and herself screaming at one another like a pair of fishwives. Across the street a tall man was walking slowly up the hill; he carried a briefcase and an elderly dog trailed behind him on a lead. She wanted to run after him, call out, force him to turn round and be Miles: 'Hullo, darling, look, hang on to this damned canine for a minute, I'm dead beat . . .' She stood and watched the figure until it disappeared out of sight round the corner by the tube station, then continued slowly up the hill. Perhaps she would give Pol a ring, say she was sorry, make it up. Then she'd catch the early train home.

* * *

'Hullo, my dear, been up in town on a spending spree?'
Someone poked Bet in the back with a brolly. Liverpool Street
station seethed, a Strauss waltz echoing merrily over the
loudspeakers. She and Pol, tearfully reunited until the next
time, had lunched in the latest Knightsbridge wine bar, and
now her headache was worse than ever. She turned crossly to
find old Monty Cornwall smiling encouragingly. 'Actually
I've been visiting my husband's grave,' she shouted above the
din, then immediately felt ashamed of herself.

Difficult filly, that, thought old Monty Cornwall, not
minding; damned good-looking, though. He squeezed Bet's
arm. 'Don't mind me, my wife says I'm always putting my
foot in it. What you need is a drink, come on, let's make for
the buffet car, I always do, it's the only decent spot on the
train.'

By the time the train pulled into Stourwick Bet had to admit
that perhaps Pete was right about Monty Cornwall. To her
surprise she'd enjoyed the journey, and Bernie, detailed to
meet her at the station by Nell ('Go carefully with her, Bern,
she'll be pretty down I expect') was a little shocked by the
sight of her smiling, animated face as she emerged from the
platform followed, he noted with disapproval, by the
ubiquitous Monty Cornwall.

'Goodbye, my dear, a most enjoyable journey. You must
come over to dinner – I'll get Kitty to ring. You and your
wife, too, of course,' Monty Cornwall turned politely to
Bernie, but Bernie was already striding towards the car.
Monty winked at Bet and raised his brolly in a gesture of
farewell. Where was Kitty, she should be waiting. Ah, there
she was. He hurried across the station yard. 'Hullo, Piggy, my
dear, bloody awful journey as usual . . . '

Bet and her son-in-law spoke little as the Renault pushed
and shoved its way out of Stourwick through the evening
rush-hour traffic. Bernie, though loth to admit it, was slightly
in awe of Bet; he never quite knew how to take her, she was so
very different to his own mother. Besides, rightly or wrongly,
and he was hard put to say why – just a gut reaction, he
supposed – he always felt she didn't appreciate his Nelly in
the way a proper mother should; call him a wimp if you like,
but that was the way he felt. For her part, Bet found Bernie

irritating but useful; he was also, annoyingly, quite often right. They rarely found themselves alone together, and when they did, as now, had little to say to each other. Particularly now, as Bet was day-dreaming about Simon Morris, and Bernie was busy trying to screw up the courage to broach the subject of a letter he'd received that morning from his dad.

Free from traffic at last, they turned off the main road into the lane that straggled haphazardly over the broad, rolling East Anglian fields to Hopton. Now or never! ('You've got to tell her, I'm not going to — they are your parents after all,' Nell had said.) And Bernie, gritting his teeth and pressing his foot hard down on the accelerator, plunged boldly in. 'I had a letter from my dad this morning, by the way. He says if it's OK by you, they'd like to come for Easter. Just a couple of days, he says, he can't spare more, but they're longing to see the place. We've more or less finished the spare room — Nell's only got to run up the curtains — and I could do with Dad's advice on the over-all heating problem.'

Oh no, not Easter! Diz away in Paris and no one to giggle with. Bet, rudely jerked out of her daydream — Simon, having been made Advertising Copywriter of the Year, had just looked deep into her eyes and asked her to dinner at the Savoy — sought despairingly for an excuse, a cop-out, some watertight reason why it would be totally out of the question to entertain Sparsworth senior and his wife for Easter, but found none. She longed to bang Bernie over the head with her rolled-up London evening paper, jump out of the car, scream. Could she, she wondered, bear it?

Reg and Maureen Sparsworth lived in a bungalow on the outskirts of Aldershot; Reg, an ex-regimental sergeant-major, having built his retirement home within, as he put it, the sound of the bugle. Small in stature like his son, Sparsworth senior possessed a formidable authority, and Bernie's obsession with efficiency undoubtedly sprang from the rigorous early training he had received from his father. Maureen Sparsworth was a large, timid lady, dragooned for so long by her husband that she'd forgotten — if indeed she ever knew — what it was like to have a mind of her own. Her two passions in life were keeping a spotlessly tidy establishment, and Bernie, and it was on these two topics only that she could be persuaded to talk. Just as well, really, as her husband seldom stopped. Apart from verbal diarrhoea, another of Reg's tiresome attributes, and there were many, was his habit of giving Bet a friendly squeeze whenever they found themselves alone together, and she still remembered with a shudder his kiss – wet and bristly – in the vestry after signing the register at the children's wedding.

'Do say if it's not on, and I'll let Dad know. I just thought it might be a good time, with Diz away in France and so on.'

Bet closed her eyes. Don't be intimidated by that family of yours, Simon had said, but that was long ago and Simon had deserted her. She didn't have any option, did she? She'd have to say yes – or rather shout it; one always shouted if one wished to be heard when driving with Bernie, for the simple reason that no matter what the prevailing circumstances, he never turned his car radio off.

'No, Bernie, that would be absolutely fine. Your mother must be excited, she'll be longing to see the house and all the work you and Nell have done. Let's just hope the weather stays fine.'

Bernie glanced at her in surprised approval. Did she mean all that, or had she been up to something in London? 'Let's hope so,' he said, 'Dad wants to nip over and have a look at Felixstowe while they're here and it won't be much fun if it pours with rain.'

It wouldn't be much fun in the sun for that matter, not with Reg Sparsworth. 'No,' Bet said, 'I suppose it wouldn't.'

After that they lapsed into silence, both deep in their own thoughts, and remained so for the rest of the journey.

Chapter Eight

'Now then, Elizabeth, sar'-major's orders; change your mind and come with us, there's a good girl. It's a lady's privilege to change her mind, you know, us men wouldn't have it any other way. We can easily squeeze you in; the wife won't mind popping in the back with the others, and we've plenty of sandwiches.'

'No, Reg, honestly,' Bet smiled palely. Would they never go? 'It's awfully kind of you, but I really do think I'd better stay at home, I still feel a bit under the weather.'

'If that's the case, Mum, I think I should stay home with you. It's not fair to leave you for so long on your own when you don't feel well.' So Nell was trying to wriggle out of it now, was she! 'I think we should leave Betty in peace,' Maureen Sparsworth added her mite. 'The weather looks none too clever, and if she doesn't feel well, sitting on a windy beach in the wet won't help.'

'I think you can leave me to be the judge of that!' Reg smiled in a way that made Bet want to scream. 'A breath of fresh air never did anyone any harm.'

Bet was alone, battling with the Sparsworths. The Redfords had chickened out, of course – golf at Le Touquet – and Diz had departed for Paris and the Duponts. The run-up to his departure (Did she think his French good enough? Were his clothes right? If the Duponts kept a servant – they were thought to be rich – should he tip same? Would he be expected to pay for anything, and if so, what? What about a dinner jacket ...?) had left her already twanging nerve-ends twanging in such a way that she felt as if someone were practising the National Anthem up and down her spinal column. She'd nevertheless waved him goodbye at Stourwick station on Maunday Thursday in a welter of misery, and the house felt drab and empty without him. Ridiculous, when you came to think about it, he'd only be away a fortnight, and the last thing she wanted was to become one of those ghastly possessive mothers.

Easter with Reg and Maureen had been every bit as bad as she thought it would be; the weather hadn't helped, and she had spent most of the time — when she wasn't cooking — vainly trying to escape from Reg. When the Felixstowe trip was first mooted, she'd pleaded incipient flu, but was pretty sure Reg suspected her of scrimshanking. She was proved right on this point when he tracked her down in the old stables, where she and Tib were hiding, for the sole purpose of telling her so. And if you asked him, her refusal to accompany them on the outing wasn't because she felt ill, but because she planned to entertain a secret lover while they were out. (She should be so lucky!) 'I've noticed a gleam in those green eyes of yours, Elizabeth, if no one else has! You can't get much past old Reg S., you know. The All-Seeing Eye, that's what the lads called me in the old days . . .'

'Look, Dad, it's gone half-past nine, if we don't start soon we'll be behind schedule.'

'Schedules are made to be broken, son, always remember that. What would have happened at Waterloo if Old Hookey had insisted on keeping to his schedule, eh?' No one answered; they weren't meant to, Reg merely wished to make the point that he was in charge and the schedule was his to do what he liked with. You couldn't have other ranks chipping in with tomfool suggestions, that would never do! All the same, the boy was right, they'd better be for the off. Pity about Elizabeth, though, he'd like to have had her sitting beside him. Those eyes, they fair gave him the jim-jams . . . come to think of it, her boobs weren't half bad either. Not to worry, there'd be other times.

'Marching orders, everyone!' Maureen cringed, Nell gritted her teeth and Bernie only just succeeded in preventing himself from jumping to attention. Only Bet looked cheerful as she rubbed a space on the wet window-pane and watched the

Sparsworth Volvo, crammed to the gunwales with people and equipment, turn smartly round in the yard, and to the accompaniment of the Sparsworth signature tune (three short, sharp toots on the horn followed by a long one − V for Victory − get it?) sweep out of the gate and disappear from view round a bend in the lane.

Blessed silence, and a whole day to do what she liked with.

The kitchen was warm, inviting, with Tib snoring in his basket, the gentle hum of the fridge, rain gurgling in the guttering outside the window, everything spotless; Maureen had seen to that before she left. The windows were clean for the first time since they'd moved in. (Have you tried Go-Go, Betty, it's ever so good, just adds that extra zip and sparkle), you could see your face in the sink, and there wasn't a cobweb in sight.

Bet poured herself a cup of coffee − another of Maureen's tips: Always have the percolator on the go, dear, you never know when the men might fancy a cup and they can get on the snappy side if they're kept waiting − and switched on Radio 2. 'Once I had a secret love . . . ' The chocolate-cream voice of Doris Day filled the kitchen. Bet, smiling, stuck her feet up on a chair, lit a cigarette, reached for the *Guardian*.

Halfway through the leader, she heard the sound of a car turning in at the gate. Oh God! She simply couldn't bear it; they must have decided not to go after all. Bet shut her eyes and began to pray . . .

'Anyone at home?' Simon's face at the window. Tib was barking, her own mouth was dry, hands shaking. 'How did you know I'd be here − the others have gone to Felixstowe −'

'I know they have − the whole village knows, and good luck to them. My word, that coffee smells good, there isn't a cup to spare, is there?'

Pull yourself together, Brandon, you're not a lovesick schoolgirl. Her hands were only trembling a little now, and she managed to pour out a coffee without Simon seeing. 'And what brings you here, Mr Morris? If it's to complain about Tib and that pheasant last week −'

'Don't be an ass. I've come to ask if you'd care to pay a visit to the Old Minster at South Elmham. I like to go there from time to time, it's good for my soul — or what little soul I have left. We could take a picnic. I know it's pouring, but we can always eat in the car, and anyway I met old Sid Garnham in the shop just now and he says it's going to clear up.'

'I've nothing to make sandwiches with,' she said, 'and I'm supposed to have flu ... What exactly is the Old Minster?'

In the end they made Marmite sandwiches; Simon said they'd been his best thing for nursery tea and he hadn't had any for years. It was his idea, too, to raid the Redford cellar for a really decent bottle of wine. 'Alfonso keeps ours under lock and key, and besides, he's in one of his moods. I'm sure your brother-in-law would be only too delighted, and we can always pay him back.'

Then they were away, bowling through the soggy spring countryside. Bet with a map on her knees; happy, not thinking of anything; not talking either, just watching the tiny blue patches in the smoke-grey clouds get larger and larger, until suddenly the blue had taken over and everything steamed in the sudden warmth of the sun. The country became flatter, a Flemish landscape; pink-washed farmhouses riding like ships in a sea of green-brown fields; here and there a solitary oak, a windmill, the square, squat tower of a village church.

'Not far now. Light me a cig, will you. See, Sid Garnham was right — he always is.'

'You haven't told me yet about the Old Minster and why it's good for your soul.' Simon puffed on his cigarette and screwed up his eyes in the sun. 'I don't suppose you've ever heard of St Fusi?' Bet shook her head. What a lot she didn't know.

'Not surprising, I suppose. As saints go, he's pretty obscure. St Fusi was the missionary priest sent from Ireland to convert East Anglia, his more famous rival being St Felix, who was sent from Rome. St Felix, after the usual vicissitudes common to that sort of work, became the first Bishop of East Anglia, with his cathedral sited somewhere near Felixstowe; exactly where isn't known. The story goes that he was joined at some point by St Fusi, hot-foot from Ireland and bursting with enthusiasm for the cause. However, although they were united in their aim to convert the wild men of East Anglia to their own, Christian God, early Christian Ireland was a very different place from world-weary Rome, and it wasn't long before the two saints fell out. As a result the bishopric was split, St Felix remaining at Felixstowe and St Fusi setting up a second, possibly rival, bishopric at South Elmham.

'Of course, a lot of all this is speculation, but we do have one overwhelming piece of evidence as to the rivalry − the Old Minster at South Elmham. And whereas there's no trace of St Felix's church − no doubt a run-of-the-mill wattle-and-daub affair, fashionable at the time and dead easy to build − the ruins of St Fusi's stone church stand to this day. We shall never know how or why he built it − and it certainly dates back to the eighth century; it was built, that's all. A huge, Romanesque edifice; a sort of poor man's St Sophia, if you like, plonked down in the middle of the Suffolk wilderness.

'No one knows, either, how long the place was used as a church − if it ever was used as a church. We do know that by the eleventh century the bishopric had removed to North Elmham in Norfolk, where there are the remains of a cathedral, although that didn't last long either and was replaced eventually by the cathedral at Norwich. Naturally, lots of legends grew up over the centuries about what the Old Minster was for. Built by a giant in a fit of madness, or as a penance; a fairy castle that somehow got left behind; Merlin's summer palace − you name it. It's only comparatively recently that anyone has taken an intelligent interest in the place, and it's surprising how few people even in Suffolk know of its existence. The tradition goes that the farmhouse on whose land it stands is built on the site of the bishop's palace, but there's no hard evidence. There's the remains of a chapel in the garden, but it's of a much later date than the Minster.

'And that's all I can tell you, really, and you no doubt think that's too much anyway. To answer your other question, Why is a visit to the Minster good for my soul? is a little more difficult. I suppose because it's beautiful, exotic, unique, forgotten, mad, probably a white elephant from the day it was built, and proves that thirteen hundred years ago there were people around every bit as daft as we are now. Oh, I don't know − do you want any more?'

'That's enough, actually.' Bet put out her hand, he took it

84

without looking at her. 'We're almost there . . .'

The last part of the journey was slow, a farm track full of potholes and puddles leading to a magnificent eighteenth-century, lime-washed farmhouse. Then, after gaining permission from the farmer to leave the car in his rick-yard, there was a muddy walk over the fields. Simon strode in front with the picnic basket and an ash wand cut from the hedge, Bet squelched along behind in her wellies, carrying the plastic bag with Pete's precious bottle of wine in it. They passed the ruined chapel, then climbed over a stile into a bumpy, sloping field full of baaing sheep. Lucky she hadn't brought Tib. Simon had said no when she suggested it. It wouldn't do him any harm to stay at home for once, he said, he could take a well-earned rest and prepare himself for the return of the sergeant-major (Bet had told Simon about the sergeant-major). At the bottom of the field they turned left along a small, boggy stream, its banks churned to mud by the sheep. Had it been as wet as this in St Fusi's time? Probably much wetter.

'Come on, slowcoach, there it is.' Simon pointed his wand — Merlin in an anorak? — towards what looked like a small wood ahead of them to the right. The trees already held a fuzz of green, one or two rather nondescript rooks flapped about, primroses shone in the bank below the trees. Just an ordinary wood, and just another of those flat, archaeological sites that have to be explained to one by an archaeologist, and which even then doesn't make sense. What had she expected, Canterbury cathedral? Simon, ahead of her, had already climbed the bank into the wood and disappeared. About to follow him, maddeningly, one of her boots got stuck in the mud, forcing her to put the bag of wine down on a nearby tussock and then hop about on one leg like an idiot in a frantic attempt to get the boot back on again. After a great deal of swearing and wondering why the hell Simon wasn't there to help, she succeeded at last, and picking up the bag of wine, prepared to follow him over the bank.

It was only then she realised that the wood wasn't a wood at all; what she'd thought to be the density of trees was in reality a huge, ruined building, the trees merely an outer ring around the grass clearing on which it stood. She clambered over the bank in a sudden rush, then just stood and looked, head back, clutching her plastic bag to her chest, mouth half-open in wonder.

How had they done it? Was it for the glory of their new-found God, or was it simply megalomania? The place looked as outlandish as a unicorn in that quiet English landscape, only much, much larger. Grey stone walls, in places still as high as the nave of a cathedral, stretched up towards the sun, arched Romanesque windows gaped blindly through matted ivy; scattered among the primroses, great blocks of stone, a Herculean pillar. There was the sudden clap and shudder of wings as a flock of pigeons, disturbed, burst from a high, creeper-covered arch and took flight towards the open sunlit fields. And Bet went on standing there. She wanted to cry; not for sadness, but not for happiness either. Simply at the sheer, unexpected wonder of the place. For a moment she even forgot Simon. Only for a moment, however. Then he was there beside her, excited, triumphant, laughing at her wonder . . . wanting her.

And she stood there, nodding, exclaiming, feeling the wind on her face, the beat of her heart; trying to pull herself together, take control of the situation.

Then, of course, it happened. It was inevitable, really, when one came to think of it. In a futile attempt to put a few more feet between herself and temptation, she took a step backwards, tripped over a tussock of grass and slithered ungracefully to the ground. Wiping the mud from her nose and feeling an absolute idiot, but otherwise OK, she looked up to find Simon kneeling beside her. 'Darling Bet, you are so utterly, absolutely, splendid, do you think I could kiss you? I'm sure the rooks won't mind, and if you're worrying about the ghost of St Fusi, there's not the slighest cause for alarm, those early saints were a broad-minded lot.'

Oh God! Why *did* he have to make her giggle? Odd how she'd never connected sex with laughter before. She became aware she was still clutching the bag of wine. 'But Simon, what shall I do with this?'

'Put it down on the grass, my love, first things first. Don't worry, we'll come to the wine later. Meanwhile . . .'

Much later — it could have been a minute, an hour or even

a century — Bet, lying on her back on the warm, damp grass, heard someone cry out. Such a strange, triumphant, happy, mournful cry. Then she felt the tears on her face, Simon's warm wetness between her legs, his limp body on her own, and knew that it was her voice that had cried out. Somewhere quite close she could hear a blackbird singing, far away the drone of a tractor. She wanted to sleep; despite the dampness, it was deliciously warm in the bed Simon had made for them in the angle of the Old Minster walls. But she mustn't sleep, there wasn't time to sleep, normality must somehow be restored. But how could normality be restored when one was lying on one's back in a fifteen-hundred-year-old church with a comparative stranger on top of one, and when one had experienced something so ... so ...

Simon stirred, rolled off her and sat up, shaking himself like a dog coming out of water. Absurdly, with the memory of their love-making still everywhere around her — it would be gone soon, she knew, like a dream one tries to retain after waking but never can — Bet found herself trying to think of something to say. In the end, all she could come up with was that she wondered what she'd done with her sweater. Simon sat up, found his and pulled it over his head. 'You're not angry with me, are you?' The words came muffled from inside the sweater.

'Of course not, why ever should I be?' she said, surprised that he should ask — this was returning to normality with a vengeance.

'That's all right, then. I only wondered. You see, some-times —'

'Sometimes what?' Jealousy, unbidden, prickled some-where deep down in her intestines.

'Sometimes after making love people get angry. Sad too — have you never heard of post-coital blues? There's a school of thought that says, the better the sex, the sadder or angrier the participants become when it's over. I suppose the reasoning behind it is that just to nip out and clean the car, or pop on your rubber gloves and do the washing-up, is rather too much of a jolt to the system after all that sublime exercise, so you burst into storms of tears or have a blazing row instead.'

'Oh,' she said, wondering about herself and Miles. She had

to admit that what rows they had were usually after sex, at least in their early days. 'If that's the case, what about you?'

'Me?' There was a pause while he found his packet of cigarettes somewhere under her left leg. 'Me, I simply try to please. And if you go on looking at me like that, Mrs Brandon, we'll never get any lunch, which would be a shame after all the trouble we took over those Marmite sandwiches.'

After lunch in a patch of sunlight at the edge of the clearing, languorous with wine, they made love again, but this time it was a gentle, sleepy thing; no angst, no urgency, no crying out. And afterwards, with Simon asleep and Bet beside him with her head on his shoulder, she felt she never wanted to think about anything again; just to exist, to be aware of the tingling of her re-awakened body, the sun on her face, was enough. Of course, such a state of things had to come to an end, she knew that, and all too soon it did. The sun, perversely, went behind a cloud, Simon woke up and looked at his watch, and it was time for them to go.

They drove home sleepily through the late afternoon sunshine, chatting desultorily of this and that, and it seemed to Bet that although what had happened at the Old Minster wasn't mentioned between them, it didn't matter, for on the whole they were at peace with each other. She wasn't absolutely sure of this, had to admit to a small, niggling doubt, but on the whole she thought they were. He did say at one point, giving her a quick sideways glance, 'That was your first time, wasn't it? I mean, you never had a lover while – '

'As it happens, no,' she said, feeling rather ashamed that she hadn't, 'there never seemed to be the time.' This made him laugh, although she hadn't intended it to, but since his laughter somehow managed to dispel the tiny spiral of tension that had unaccountably risen between them, she was glad it did. He leaned over and kissed her on the top of her head. 'You ain't 'alf a caution, Mrs Brandon, as our old nanny used to say. Who needs time, for God's sake.'

Back at Hopton, it was raining, and by the look of it had been raining all day. In the yard, horrendously, was the Sparsworth Volvo; they must have come home early because of the weather. 'Oh my God, Simon, what am I going to do now? They shouldn't be home for hours yet.'

'There's no need to panic, for a start. Why shouldn't they be back, poor things, if it's been raining like this at Felixstowe I don't blame them. I —'

'There you are, you naughty minx! Flu, my arse — if you'll pardon the expression. Why don't you bring the boyfriend in for a cuppa? I'll pop the kettle on, it won't take a jiffy.' Reg, grinning like a horse-collar, was waving a tea-towel out of the kitchen window. Rain was pouring down, the dog was barking . . .

'Simon, *please* come in with me, you must — I simply can't face them all on my own.'

'Oh, don't be such a baby, of course you can.' Simon was laughing so much he could barely speak, only splutter and hold on to the steering-wheel. At any other time she would have thought it funny too. 'Look, I'd love to join the sar'-major for a brew-up, but you see I promised old Cyn I'd be back by six.'

'You bastard, you cowardly, feeble, traitorous bastard!'

'Don't forget your picnic basket, and let me know about the wine, I don't want you to get into trouble —'

'Bugger the wine!' Bet snatched the picnic basket and slammed the car door as hard as she could. 'A bientôt.' Simon, still laughing, gave a quick thumbs-up sign to the goggling Reg, blew Bet a kiss and roared out of the yard. Seething, she watched him go.

'Come on in out of the rain, dear,' said Reg from the shelter of the back door, 'you look worse than I feel . . .'

Chapter Nine

'We would like to have stayed an extra day, dear, we really would' — Maureen whisking through the washing-up next morning, her pink rubber gloves a blur in the foaming, fairy liquid — 'but Reg has this meeting tonight. He must be there, he says; if he isn't, they might do something he wouldn't like.'

So would I if I were them. 'I do understand, Maureen, I'm only sorry you couldn't have seen Diz — but perhaps another time.'

'Come along now, girls, no yacking! We must be on the road in half an hour. I want to get away a bit early, I promised I'd pop in at Sid Kettle's garage on the way and give him that address.' (Lucky old Sid Kettle).

To Bet's surprise Reg had appeared to accept her explanation of the previous day's change of plan — she'd suddenly felt better, the sun had come out, Simon had appeared unexpectedly — entirely at its face value. 'Had a picnic, then, did you, you and young what's-his-name?'

'Simon Morris, actually. Yes, it was so nice and sunny by that time, we thought ... why not?'

'Bloody cold on the beach,' he'd said, forgetting to pardon the expression. But 'Picnic, my arse', he'd confided to Maureen in the privacy of the spare bedroom, 'that's not what I'd call it.'

In fact Bet's arrival home at the end of that extraordinary afternoon had turned out to be something of an anticlimax. It reminded her of her first weekend at her parents' house after losing her virginity — she and Miles thrashing about on the lumpy old divan in that bedsitter she had in Chelsea Manor

90

Street; the gas fire had run out halfway through, and Miles, naked, stubbed his toe quite badly in the dark trying to find a sixpence to put in the meter. Proud of her newfound womanhood — amazingly, she had thought like that in those days — she was sure her mother would notice the change in her at once; an extra glow perhaps, a certain languor. Didn't mums always know? But this mum hadn't, she'd just carried on as normal, and Bet, although relieved, had also been a little disappointed. And now it was the same. Ludicrous, when one came to think of it — did one ever grow up?

The Sparsworths left at last, the junior branch having departed for work a couple of hours before. Maureen waved tearfully out of the Volvo window and Reg kissed her goodbye, his moustache tickling her nose and making her want to sneeze. 'Mind how you go then, girl, and don't do anything I wouldn't do,' he whispered, giving her bottom a friendly pinch and looking at her a little too searchingly for comfort. Bet yawned and smiled and yawned again, and prayed for them to hurry up and go, and for the phone to ring. She'd slept little the previous night; really, in fact, she had simply lain in bed waiting for it to be time to get up.

Perversely, however, the utter silence that followed their departure was almost uncanny; she'd never known the place so quiet. She would have liked the radio, but if she were upstairs sorting out the Sparsworth bedroom — not that there was anything to sort out, Maureen had seen to that, even put her and Reg's sheets ready for washing in the machine — she might not hear the telephone. She looked at her watch, she'd been looking at it ever since nine o'clock — so what? Eleven-thirty. Surely Simon should have rung by now? Perhaps he'd been unable to get through; perhaps their phone was out of order. It had been on the blink, now she came to think of it, for weeks. She hurried into the hall and picked up the receiver, only to be met with the dialling tone buzzing mockingly in her ear. 'I'm ready and waiting,' it seemed to say, 'if people don't want to use me that's their look-out.'

When it did finally make up its mind to ring, about half an hour later, she only just heard it above the Hoover. She was upstairs, giving Diz's bedroom a going-over. Quite un-necessary, and he'd be furious if she moved any of his things, but one had to do something. She tore downstairs, mouth dry, heart beating, tripped over Tib who'd placed himself strategically at the bottom for that very purpose, sprinted across the hall minus a shoe, only to discover it wasn't Simon at all. It wasn't even Pete, but some dim-witted girl selling double-glazing.

After that, she knew with the absolute certainty born of despair that Simon wasn't going to ring. To be honest, he hadn't actually said he would, indeed he had arranged no further meeting. But what with Reg butting in when they got back yesterday, and all that rain, he never really had a chance to. That was why she had been so sure he would ring this morning. She had been so sure that during the course of her long, sleepless night she had rehearsed — using, she now realised in the cold light of day, every cliché in the book — what she would say to him when he did. How she felt they should go carefully before making any decision about the future, how she had been so unprepared for what happened that she had had no time to assess her feelings, and no doubt he hadn't either. And so on and so on. Make a decision about the future — was she mad? They were nowhere near that stage yet, quite possibly never would be. Simon, she was sure, was the last person to spend his time making decisions about the future, Simon . . .

Simon is a person who plays games with people.

Unbidden the words jumped into her head from now-here — and were immediately repudiated. What did she know of people who played games with people? Mercifully, in her so far protected and uneventful life — and she was beginning to realise just how protected and uneventful her life had been — nothing; she had never encountered such people. Read about them, yes, heard about them, yes. If Miles were to be believed, the Civil Service was absolutely jam-packed with them. But she herself had never known one. To be the object of such people's games, though, one surely must be involved, quite deeply involved, with them before their games could work? And she wasn't deeply involved with Simon — well, not yet, not exactly. There was, however, no earthly point in denying that she was most terribly attracted by him, and found him funny, intriguing and good company to boot. And

92

wanted to see him again, wanted that very much indeed. But above all, she wanted some sort of reassurance from him that the step she'd taken yesterday at the Old Minster — for her so great, for him possibly no more than routine — had been the right step; hurting no one, betraying no one, not even Miles.

And there, of course, was the crunch. Still standing by the telephone, she extracted a cigarette from the packet in her trouser pocket, lit it, and willed herself to think about Miles. She'd tried to think about him last night; bring him back to her, however briefly, in the way she had been able to since within a few weeks of his death; but she had failed miserably. She'd been too tired, too tense, and perhaps she hadn't really wanted to face up to him anyway. But today was different, today she knew that she must. She shut her eyes and thought about Miles so hard it hurt. What would he feel about Simon? Would he feel betrayed? That she'd cheapened the memory of their marriage by allowing, indeed wanting, another man to make love to her so soon? A man so different to himself, a man who . . .

'Darling, for heaven's sake who d'you think I am? If you're going to spend the rest of your life racked with guilt every time you look at another man, let's face it, it's not going to be much of a life, is it?' Outside in the garden a pair of magpies hooked worms from a patch of grass under the hall window; Bet watched them through the smoke of her cigarette, a watery smile on her face. Miles's presence was all round her now; his special brand of common sense, slightly acerbic humour and love washing over her in a warm, comforting stream, revitalising her as it had done so often during their life together.

He was right, as always. Of course there was no need for her to feel guilty. And if feeling guilty was making her behave like a jilted teenager, it was high time she stopped feeling guilty. All this rubbish about people playing games with one another — pure paranoia! There were no doubt a hundred perfectly good reasons why Simon hadn't rung, and if she was so desperate to make contact, why not ring him? She thought about this for a moment and then decided not to. She didn't, for a start, know Smike McGregor's number, and Simon probably wouldn't want her to ring him at work anyway —

93

Miles hated to be rung at work — and besides, what on earth would she say? OK then, she wouldn't ring him, at least that was settled.

But it was about the only thing that was settled, and she was still left with this overpowering urge to do *something* — issue a statement to the Press, publish a poem, make a speech, scream — anything but just fiddle around with the Hoover waiting for the bloody phone to ring. It was then, just as the two magpies flew away in a sudden noisy blurr of black and white, to be replaced by a rather tatty sparrow, that the idea came to her.

She would give a party!

Why not, and what could be simpler? After all, she did owe several people hospitality, including Cyn Westover. She could ring the Manor, issue a verbal invitation casually including Simon, and *voilà*. Simon would naturally accept — well, if he didn't at least she would know where she stood — and everything would then be out in the open with no more of this absurd hole-and-corner stuff. What's more, he and the children would be able to meet properly, and who knew, once they got to know him better they might even come to like him. In fact the possibilities of the whole idea was absolutely boundless . . .

What about trying for next Saturday? It would have to be at a weekend, and the sooner the better. Bernie could organise the drink, Nell would at last have a chance to make those wretched tuna fish vol-au-vents she was always on about, Diz could . . . Seething with plans and excitement, she finished the first cigarette, lit a second and decided to ring the Manor there and then, before she lost her nerve.

''Allo, 'Opton eight-four-nine?' Oh God, bloody Alfonso! She'd forgotten about Alfonso. 'Yo ablo Senorita Westover, por favor?' She'd gone to evening classes in Spanish one winter at the City Lit', thinking it would be useful on holiday. Somehow it hadn't been, no one ever seemed to understand what she was saying. The silence at the other end of the line was deafening. Then a click and a different voice. 'Yes?'

'Oh . . . Miss Westover, it's you. Betty Brandon here.'

'And what can I do for you, Mrs Brandon?' She hated people who said that, there wasn't really any proper answer one could give; anyway, it made one feel small. 'Well, actually I was wondering whether you would like to drop in for a drink on Saturday evening, and ... and do of course bring anyone who might be staying.'

'Adore to, my dear, and most kind of you to suggest it, but afraid no can do. I'm off to the States on Thursday for three weeks. Si could probably make it, I'll ask him. He's gone back to London, but he'll be down while I'm away, he's promised to caretake. He's taking some time off work – whether off his own bat or Smike McGregor's one doesn't enquire. Says he's going to make a start on his book, but as he's been going to do that for more years that I like to remember, I have my doubts. Anyway, even if he does actually get down to it, I'm sure he could take a break and come to your party. He did so enjoy taking you to the Old Minster yesterday – splendid spot, isn't it? Look, my dear, must fly. I've a host of things to do before Thursday. 'Bye.'

Bet, feeling sick, sat down on an adjacent chair. So Simon had told his precious cousin about their love-making, had he. No doubt they'd enjoyed a good laugh together, discussed the whole thing in detail. Don't be absurd, Brandon, you're being paranoid again. Of course they didn't discuss it in detail, why ever should they. She swallowed, trying, not wholly success-fully, to regain her earlier confidence – and Tib, seeing the state she was in, jumped on her knee and licked her face. She kissed the top of his head and sat there fondling his ears, wondering what to do next. Well, if she really intended to give a party – and it seemed she was committed to do just that – she'd better pull herself together and invite a few people. Now, what about Old Monty Cornwall ...?

The guest list, when completed, was, to say the least, unimpressive. Desperate, she'd been reduced to asking the vicar and his wife. Yes, he and Angela would be delighted, he'd shouted down the phone and Bet, surprised at his enthusiasm, added the Snatelys' name to her list. It was only afterwards she wondered if he had thought her someone else. He was known to be rather deaf ...

And of course Ron and Emmie Stokes. She'd first met Ron Stokes, a tall, elderly, skeletally thin man with a suspect smile, who wore sandals all the year round and never drew breath, when he appeared in the vegetable garden one afternoon with a petition. Developers, he said, were seeking the Council's permission to build on Church Green and must, at all costs, be prevented. He was sure she would agree; he only had to look at her, he said, to know she was one of us; he knew these things, people had an aura. Bet, in her wellies, mud on her nose, sowing broad beans in the damp, clay soil – like trying to plant currants in uncooked chocolate sponge – had not wanted to talk to anyone, let alone Ron Stokes. Smiling too eagerly because she felt guilty, she said, 'How awful, of course I'll sign, Mr –?'

'Oh, call me Ron, everyone does.' Much cheery laughter on Ron's part when a gust of wind blew the petition out of his hand and Tib stood on it. 'I'm not afraid of a peck of healthy mud, my dear, and I'll wager you aren't either.' His little eyes flickered down the front of her tweed jacket – the ancient one with the tear in the elbow which Diz said made her look like Worzel Gummidge – and rested meditatively on the curve of her breasts. 'Come to tea, my dear, drop in at any time, my wife Emmie and I keep open house. It must be lonely for you here.'

Luckily she was saved by the phone. 'I'll have to dash, I'm afraid, my sister from London – she'll talk for hours, she always does ...' She wasn't, however, saved from tea, Emmie Stokes saw to that. She rang the very next morning. 'My hubby was so delighted to meet a kindred spirit, Mrs Brandon, it quite made his day. He gets a little lonely sometimes, Hopton's so different to Singapore – that's where we used to live. Our bungalow is opposite Kettle's garage – The Haven – you can't miss it.'

So Bet had gone, and they'd had sponge cake that melted in the mouth and two sorts of tea, in a room full of fumed oak, Benares brass, bamboo tables and Buddhas. Afterwards Ron had taken her into his inner sanctum, and they had stood pressed uneasily together in a tiny room the size of a broom cupboard, while Ron explained the mysteries of transcendental meditation. By the time he'd finished, Bet felt she was about to pass out, and Ron's eyes were beginning to glaze over and his breath was coming in short, sharp pants ...

One good thing about having the Stokes, at least she'd get them over with — she had been brought up strictly on the manners front; one always, no matter what, returned hospitality. God knew what Simon would make of them. She felt like Lizzy Bennett arranging a party for Mr Darcy, with no one to come but Mr Collins, Mrs Bennett and her own frightful sisters. This made her giggle, and she was still giggling when Emmie Stokes came on the line. Emmie Stokes sounded stunned by the invitation. Did no one ever ask them out? Probably not. She added their name to her list.

'Now, Bet, are you having caterers, because if you are — '

'For Christ's sake, Pol, who d'you think I am? Of course I'm not having caterers.'

'It was only a thought, there's no need to be rude. Honestly, I don't know what's got into you lately. You ring me to say you've invited half the county to a party — I confess that at first I did think the idea a tiny bit on the ambitious side, but fun all the same — then you jump down my throat when I ask about caterers. It was only that Kitty Cornwall told me the people to have are Thrush and Co, they — '

'Where you get the idea that I've invited half the county I cannot imagine. There are at most a dozen people coming, and I doubt if all of them will turn up. The only food provided will be a few crisps and a packet or two of nuts from the Post Office. Do I make myself clear?'

Pol dialled Pete's office. 'Pete, I simply cannot cope with Bet at all over this party; she's insisting on inviting all these people and then flatly refusing to give them anything to eat. It makes one wonder what she'll be offering them to drink — a thimbleful of cooking sherry if her present attitude is anything to go by.' Pete closed his eyes; he'd only just got back from a meeting with old Bollocks and some turd from the Treasury. It had gone on and on, and quite frankly he couldn't take much more. 'Don't worry, ducky, I'm sure Bet knows what she's doing. Anyway, from what she told me — '

'I see, she's already been in touch with you, has she?'

'I rang her this morning to thank her for the invitation, that's all. And from what I can gather, there's only going to be a handful of people – that meditation chap from the village, the vicar, Simon Morris –'

'If you ask me, that's what the party's in aid of ...'

Diz, newly returned from his trip to Paris, showed little interest in the forthcoming party. His Easter in France had transformed his way of thinking completely, he told his mother, and he was now a dedicated francophile. Never in his life, he said – for the umpteenth time – had he met such interesting, kind, amusing, civilised people as the Duponts.

'And rich with it.' Bernie had grown tired of listening to minute descriptions of meals eaten, art galleries visited – whose owners Monsieur Dupont naturally numbered amongst his most intimate friends – and gatherings backstage at the Comedie Francaise. Diz waved his arms about. 'Can't you get it into your thick, insular head, it's not the money – although I admit the Duponts' place is pretty luxurious – it's their whole way of life.' He glanced round the kitchen, seeking inspiration. 'It's ... well, it's not like this.'

'I never for one moment thought it would be,' interrupted his mother tartly, 'and what I wonder is, if *chez Dupont* is as wonderful as you say, what are we going to do with Jean-Pierre when he comes here in July? He'll be bored stiff.'

'No he won't, Mum. You just don't understand. JP's one hell of a nice guy. He takes his pleasures where he finds them – he won't mind in the least what the place is like. But there is one thing, while we're on the subject –'

'When are we ever off it?' – Bernie's parting shot as he whizzed out of the back door on his way to give the lawn a quick once-over with the new hover. 'Oh belt up, cretin. Have you any idea what a pain you are?' Diz turned to his mother. 'As I was saying, Mum, there is just one thing ...'

'Yes?' Why did one have children?

'It's JP's sister, Liza. I mentioned her in my postcard, she's at the Sorbonne. I was just wondering – that is, the Duponts were wondering – whether you could possibly see your way to having her to stay too, just for JP's first week. The Duponts would pay, of course, and she's dead keen to visit England.'

So that's how it was! It had to come sometime, she

98

supposed, and she couldn't complain, could she, when she herself . . .? She kissed him on the top of his head. 'I'm sure that can be arranged, darling. I only hope Liza won't be bored and the weather's good . . .' But Diz had already disappeared upstairs to write to Madame Dupont assuring her that all was well, Liza could come too.

By Saturday morning Bet had still heard nothing from Simon. No news was, hopefully, good news, but she had nevertheless slept little, eaten less, and was, so everyone kept telling her, bad-tempered in the extreme. Diz was despatched to the post office to buy crisps, Bernie had collected the drink from Victoria Wine in Stotleigh, and Nell had done the much vaunted tuna fish mixture for putting in the vol-au-vent cases she'd made the night before. Unfortunately these had not turned out quite as expected, too little butter perhaps. Never mind, she told Bet optimistically, once they'd been filled no one would notice. Bet shrugged her shoulders gloomily — who cared anyway?

'Mum,' Nell's voice was uncharacteristically sharp, 'it was your idea to have this party in the first place, in fact you absolutely insisted on it. I do think you might at least try and show a little enthusiasm.'

'I'm sorry, darling, it's just that I haven't been sleeping too well lately — you've all been wonderful, you really have.' And hoping she sounded suitably enthusiastic, but doubting it, Bet hurried away to polish the furniture.

Later, exhausted by all their preparations, Bet, the children and Bernie were just sitting down to a late lunch of sausages and baked potatoes — Diz's favourites, despite his views on the inadequacy of English cooking — when Pol suddenly appeared in the doorway. 'Sorry to interrupt,' she looked disapprovingly round the untidy kitchen, 'but I've brought a small contribution to the party.' Blushing a little, she plonked a large hamper on the table amongst the cooling sausages. 'Just a few bits and pieces,' she said, not looking at anyone. 'Fortnum's do a special party pack.'

They opened the box with trembling fingers. Predictably, it contained absolutely everything anyone — even Madame Dupont herself — could possible have wished for to titillate the appetite of the most jaded party-goer.

'What price cardboard vol-au-vents now, eh?' said Diz, unpacking a small tin of truffles. 'Pol, you shouldn't have, it must have cost the earth. Mr Snately will think I've gone mad – truffles and caviar ... Pol, *really*.' For an absurd moment Bet thought she might burst into tears – she seemed to be so emotional these days – but instead she kissed her gratified sister and patted her shoulder. 'I've half a mind to keep it all for us. It's wasted on the people coming to this party.'

The Stokes were the first to arrive, followed precisely three minutes later by the Snatelys. Bet and Diz had to cope on their own; Nell said she couldn't come until she'd dealt with the sausages, and Bernie said he was still putting the last-minute touches to his bar, and why did people have to come so early? Not for Bernie Pete's vague but lavish hospitality, at whose parties it was sometimes possible to find oneself consuming a glass of neat gin, the host having been distracted by something while pouring it out. Bernie's bottles were arrayed in serried ranks, his glasses sparkled, each drink would be carefully measured according to the rules of the licensing trade.

The Stokes and Snatelys knew one another, of course, but that was about as far as it went. Mr Snately disapproved of meditation, and Mrs Snately, a huge woman with blue hair and a mean mouth, was saving her energy for the next arrivals, rightly concluding that she hadn't been forced to turn out on a chilly evening like this simply to meet the Stokes.

'Caviar, Mrs Snately?' Diz, the son of the house, smiled boyishly. 'Good gracious, Desmond – it is Desmond, isn't it, such an unusual name – I haven't eaten caviar since the bishop's daughter married young Quentin Merrivale. Of course she's married to someone else now, but I never can remember her second husband's name. What's Ophelia Merrivale's new husband called, Horace?' she roared at the vicar, who was standing in front of the fire, glass in hand, opening and shutting his eyes like an owl blinded in sudden daylight.

'What's that, dear?'

'Ophelia Merrivale, what's her new name?'

'Ophelia who?'

Bet hovered uncertainly in the background. She longed to escape; this was not the party she had visualised. What in hell's name was Nell up to, it couldn't take that long to cook a few sausages. Where were the Redfords? She took a gulp at her gin and tonic.

'What beautiful things you have here, Betty. I appreciate beautiful possessions as much as the next man, but beauty of the spirit is what I'm really after.' Ron Stokes put his hand on her shoulder, smiling roguishly. 'It's no use having good furniture out East,' said Emmie Stokes, her newly lacquered, deep auburn perm sparkling in the lamplight, her floral two-piece hung about with beads, 'the ants eat it.'

'Oh dear, what a frightful nuisance. Would you like some caviar?'

'Not for me, dear, if you don't mind. Fish roes disagree with me. It's been the same ever since a holiday we spent in Bognor years ago. We stayed in a boarding-house behind the station — of course, it's been pulled down now — and the landlady gave us cod's roe for every meal. Do you remember, dear?' Bet was pleased to see a spasm of annoyance flicker across Ron's face. However, no doubt used to such deflationary tactics on the part of his wife, he quickly rose to the occasion. 'Emmie, my dear,' he sounded as though he were talking to a wayward infant, 'this is caviar, the food of kings and princes, it's not the same thing at all. I can see our Betty here must have friends in high place — '

'Can I press you to one of Bernie's specials, sir?' *Sir?* 'It helps to wash down the caviar.'

'My dear young man — Damien, isn't it? I've been so looking forward to meeting you, your mother has ...'

Bet fled. Would Simon never come?

But the caviar was all but eaten and they were on to the vol-au-vents and chipolatas before Bet, stuck with Emmie Stokes — 'I don't care what people say, I do like a bit of colour in my garden, don't you, dear?' — heard the front door bell and knew, all her other guests having arrived, that this time it must be Simon. Feeling the beginning-to-be-familiar lurch in her stomach, and mumbling an excuse to Emmie, she made a dash for the hall, only to find Pete had forestalled her. 'Ah, Bet, here's Morris at last, says he's walked all the way from the Manor. I've told him he's missed the caviar, but he says no problem, he doesn't like the stuff anyway.'

'Can't "Morris" speak for himself?' Suddenly Bet felt in command – or almost. At least he'd come, and to walk all the way from the Manor showed a certain determination.

'Sorry to be late, Titania, but on such a night one really had to walk. Actually, it was rather a case of needs must, my car's playing up again. I used the short cut through the wood so I'm afraid my shoes are in a bit of a mess.'

'Nature-lover, are you?' Pete was still hovering. While Simon bent down to get the mud off his shoes, Bet gave Pete a quick kick on the shins. 'In case you've forgotten, Pete, this happens to be my party.'

'No need to be like that, ducky, I was just standing in until you arrived. I must say you arrived pretty quickly – not gone on the chap, are you?' Drink always made Pete reckless. 'And why does he call you Titania?'

'Because we met in a wood, Redford, does that satisfy you?' Simon had given up trying to clean his shoes. 'And in anticipation of your next question, no, I haven't yet worked out what my role is. When I do, I'll be sure to let you know.'

Pete looked at him, his mouth slightly open. 'Whisky do you?'

'Admirably, how did you guess?' Pete went.

'God, I look like the wild man of Borneo.' Simon peered at himself in the hall mirror. 'You haven't a comb on you, Titania?'

'No, but you can borrow the dog's comb if you like,' Bet said, searching the face's reflection for something, she didn't quite know what – knew only that the something, whatever it was, wasn't there. 'You could have rung.'

'I fully intended to, I really did.' The eyes, meeting Bet's in the mirror, were veiled, the wary eyes of a practised lover, looking her over, giving nothing away. 'But what with one thing and another this week's been an absolute pig. Things got rather on top of me and – '

'They have a habit of doing that? Things – getting on top of you?' She was surprised at the acid in her voice. This was not how she'd visualised their meeting.

'*Touché*!' Simon gave a bark of laughter and the brown eyes looking into hers widened in surprise, vulnerable, acknowledging a hit, seeing her, perhaps for the first time, as an equal. 'I deserved that.' Somewhere, something deep down in Bet breathed a sigh of relief. 'I only thought – '

'And you were right, my love, you were right.' He turned away from the mirror and put his hands on her shoulders. 'Now tell me frankly, without resorting to the dog's comb, am I tidy enough to meet your guests?'

And then, for no particular reason, they started to giggle. They were still doing this when Diz appeared at Bet's elbow; suspicious, not really wanting to be friendly, but determined to be correct – so like his father. 'Hullo, sir, can I get you a drink or is my mother looking after you?'

Your uncle is, or so he promised, but thanks for the offer. Incidentally, the name's Simon. Being addressed as 'sir' by a member of the younger generation makes me feel a hundred.'

'I've no desire to do that, sir ... I mean, Simon. It's just that we were rather strictly brought up, I suppose, but I'll try to remember in future. Did your car break down?'

'No, I walked – took the short cut through the wood, but it turned out to be further than I remembered.'

Bet watched the hostility flicker between them, it both frightened and excited her. Was this what power felt like? 'Come on, Simon, now you're here at last, let me introduce you to a few people, we can't spend the evening standing in the hall, it's too cold.'

'Mum, the Snatelys are about to leave. Mrs Snately's looking for you to say goodbye.' Diz, who'd been chewing an olive stone, took the stone out of his mouth, tossed it into a nearby ash tray and turned to Simon 'Nice to have met you ... er ... Simon, but I must dash. I promised Bern I'd get some more ice from the Redford fridge. See you later, perhaps.'

Simon looked after him. 'What a very well-behaved boy, Titania, he surely does you credit. You – ' But before he could continue he was engulfed by Kitty Cornwall. 'Si, how are you? We never had a chance to talk the other night, and I so wanted to ask you about the dog in that chocolates commercial of yours. How on earth did they manage to make it do that?'

'All a trick, Kitty, you gullible old thing. And it's not my commercial, I simply had one small hand in it. You see ...'

Bet left them to it.

And after that, somewhat to her surprise and, she had to admit, her slight disappointment – she'd expected at least some small display of fireworks from him – Simon's party behaviour was exemplary. With the exception of her own family, who remained obstinately and inexplicably impervious to his particular brand of upper-crust charm, he was plainly considered by her ill-assorted guests to be the evening's star attraction – members of the Westover family were seldom seen at village gatherings of this sort, and Simon never. However, from her own little orbit – it was extraordinary how easy it was to switch to automatic pilot on these occasions, at one point she'd even agreed to let the garden be used for this year's village fête – Bet watched his antics with irritation. Admittedly, he did wink at her once over the top of Angie Snately's hat – she'd stayed on, of course – but that was the only contact between them until he suddenly came up behind her in the old pantry, where she'd fled to fetch a floor-cloth. Tib, having pinched a plate of Nell's tuna fish vol-au-vents, had regurgitated the whole lot all over the sitting-room carpet.

'"And greasy Joan doth keel the pot"! Are you trying to avoid me?'

'No, of course I'm not,' Bet, unnerved, went on ringing out the floorcloth.

'Do leave that wretched thing alone, Titania, and look at me.' He spun her round so she was facing him. Obviously a little drunk – not too drunk, just a little – he looked, Bet thought, like a dissipated Italian film star. 'The Cornwalls are giving me a lift back to the Manor, so I must go. We can't talk here, anyway, with all this riff-raff about. What about lunch on Monday?'

What indeed? But lunch on Monday didn't mean just lunch on Monday, did it? Oh, to hell with it! Why shouldn't she have some fun sometimes, everyone else did. Besides, he was looking at her in that way again; the way that made it more or less impossible not to accept.

She let out a long sigh. 'All right then,' she said, noticing he wore gold cuff-links and that they had a crest on them. 'Your place or mine?'

'That's my girl!' Simon took the hand that wasn't holding the floorcloth and gently kissed it. 'I thought perhaps yours, if that's OK by you, then we could finish the leftovers.'

And that was when it really started.

'Seems a nice enough chap, if you like that type,' Pete said to his wife over a tough steak at The George. 'Can't understand what all the fuss has been about. He and Bet hardly spoke all evening.'

'It's no good, Pete, I simply cannot eat this steak. It'll have to be sent back to the kitchens; these people mustn't be allowed to get away with such slipshod cooking ...'

'And what did you think of Mum's boyfriend, then?' Nell to Bernie, as they bounced about in their brand new Heals bed.

'Not a lot, if you really want to know.' They were trying a new position and Bernie needed all his concentration for the job in hand.

'I do hope Si Morris isn't after that nice Brandon woman,' said Kitty Cornwall, putting the finishing touches to her rollers and preparing to climb between the sheets, 'because if he is ...'

But old Monty Cornwall was already asleep.

Chapter Ten

Sunday was got through somehow, with everyone, as usual after a party, thoroughly bad-tempered. Bet was much the same. Odd, this; surely she ought to be full of effervescence, prancing about metaphorically speaking, on cloud nine? Wasn't that how one was supposed to feel at the start of an affair? Well, she didn't, and there it was, although she did admit to a sort of ice-cold shivering excitement whenever she thought about Monday. Things weren't helped by the fact that she and Nell had a row. Rows with Nell were fairly rare these days, but they did still happen ocassionally.

This one was over washing-powder, or rather the lack of it. Deciding to do the weekly wash on Sunday — this particular Monday promising to be altogether too fraught for such a mundane domestic chore — Bet found her plan frustrated by the infuriating discovery that although she had bought a new packet of soap powder, jumbo sized, only three days before, they were already out of it. The fact that this was always happening, because of Nell's scarcely credible prodigality with the stuff — Bet sometimes wondered if she didn't supplement Bernie's diet with it — only added fuel to the flames of her wrath. And Nell's excuse, that perhaps Bet's generation wasn't quite so hot on hygiene as Nell's, because of being brought up during the war and having to learn to do without, merely added insult to injury.

Why, she wondered as she turned the roast potatoes and burned her fingers on the baking tin, when one was going through the vast emotional changes one was going through, did one have to be so continually bogged down by irritating trivia?

Mercifully the Redfords were out all day, having lunch with some of their posh friends, and she only saw Pol for a quick sisterly peck on the cheek before they left for London in the evening. No one mentioned Simon — whether by design or otherwise, Bet wasn't sure. She couldn't help wishing they *had* mentioned him, even thought any remark they made would almost certainly have infuriated her.

Sunday came to an end at last, and then it was Monday. Thank God she'd told Simon not to arrive before twelve-thirty! Christine Barnet always stayed until twelve-fifteen on Mondays, later if she spent too much time gossiping with Bet. And this morning, what with the party, there did happen to be an awful lot to gossip about, so that by the time Christine said, 'Gracious, I must go, I said I'd be home early and give Dad his dinner, it's Mum's day for the hospital', Simon was due to arrive at any minute, and Bet had to dash round like a maniac, getting everything ready.

She needn't have bothered; by the time he did arrive, nearly an hour late, she'd consumed an entire packet of salted peanuts, drunk two glasses of sherry, and decided he'd got cold feet and wasn't coming after all. She was out in the vegetable garden, checking whether any more broad beans had emerged — she had to do something — when he appeared at last, a bottle of wine under one arm and a rather tired-looking fern in a pot under the other.

'What on earth's that?' She pointed to the tired-looking fern. Not what she'd meant to say, but the sherry was beginning to work.

'Some sort of fern, it was the only thing I could find in the greenhouse that seemed suitable. Old Tom appears to have given up pot plants.'

'Old Tom?'

'Our gardener.'

'Won't he be livid, you pinching one of his ferns?'

'I doubt whether he'll notice. He must be ninety if he's a day. But Alfonso was livid about the wine. He refused point-blank to give me the key of the cellar, that's why I'm so late, we had a bit of a barney. He always plays up when Cyn's away.'

'But you got it?'

'Oh yes, I got it, I usually do − get things, I mean − if I make up my mind to.'

'Should I be impressed?' Again the look of surprise she had noticed on the night of the party; this time his surprise was mixed with a barely detectable flash of annoyance. What supine women he must go in for!

'No, just stating a fact. And before we go any further, may I say how very pretty you look, standing there in your wellies among the sprouting cabbages − or are they marrows?'

'Broad beans, in fact. Being a member of the ruling class and having a gardener, I suppose one can afford to be so ignorant. Anyway, come and have some lunch, that's what you're here for, isn't it, and if we don't get a move on the kids will be home. Look, I'll take the fern in case you drop it.'

But they never got round to lunch, or not the one she'd planned. Somewhere on the way to see to it, other things beyond their control took over. And instead of making for the kitchen, arms entwined they were climbing the stairs to her bedroom.

And after that the other things took over altogether.

'What about lunch, then?' A long time later, Simon, sitting up in bed, reached for a cigarette. 'Christ, it's nearly three, won't things start happening soon?'

'Not for a bit. Actually, I don't think I could eat anything just at the moment.' Bet lay naked beside him, her body warm, exhausted, at peace. And her soul? She wasn't too sure about her soul, but decided on balance to leave worrying about that until later. Meanwhile ...

Simon looked down at her, one eye screwed up against the smoke from his cigarette. 'I believe you enjoyed that, Titania; that I did goes without saying. I always thought under that decorous façade there was one real, wild woman trying to get out.'

'Do I have a decorous façade? It's the first I've heard of it. Is that why you wanted to go to bed with me − to find out if you were right?'

'And I took you for an intelligent woman! I make love because I love making love, not to find out things; that's why it always works.'

'What a conceited creature you are! What do you mean, always works?'

Simon stubbed out his cigarette. 'I mean, always works. And as you don't seem interested in lunch, what about another demonstration ...?'

And for three whole weeks it was like that, the pattern set on the first day, weekends and the remainder of Bet's life to be got through as best she could. It was for her three weeks of discovery, angst, elation, guilt, enchantment, fear, and all the other things in between. I've become a hedonist, she told herself proudly as she worked in her garden − rampant now in the warmth of early May − or took Tib for his daily walk in a countryside which, despite pesticides, prairie farming and ditches full of empty fertilizer bags, remained almost overpowering in its spring freshness and beauty. Simon, the magician, the wizard met in the woods − Oberon surely, not Bottom? − had shown her the way. How to become, in fact rather than just in principle − she'd always been one in principle, or liked to think so − the liberated woman everyone talked and wrote about. Free, uncommitted, loving sex for its own sake, not for the love of her partner. Mistress of her soul, captain of her fate.

And yet, and yet − and this was where the angst came in − as the days wore on she was increasingly, disturbingly aware that, far from becoming more liberated, she was becoming less so by the minute. In other words, she was breaking all the rules, she was getting too fond of Simon; although obsessed might better describe the way she felt, as she seemed to spend most of her waking hours thinking about him. If, only a few short weeks ago, someone had asked her whether she thought it possible she could be in this state over a man several years her junior with whom she had almost nothing in common, she would have laughed in his face. Chastened, she knew better now. It was, alas, only too possible, and there was little she could do about it but live from day to day and hope, none too optimistically, for the best.

And what of Simon's feelings for her? Ridiculous to have to admit that she had no idea how he felt, but she didn't. 'This is going to be fun, Titania, I promise. No regrets. No tears?' he'd said, his voice uncharacteristically anxious, as they

109

kissed goodbye at the end of that first afternoon, and she'd nodded reassuringly. If non-commitment was the order of the day, then so be it, and who was she to complain? But despite his words, sometimes — when he thought she wasn't looking — she would catch a light in his eyes that surely wasn't mere lust, or the spirit of easy camaraderie that had grown up between them in their efforts to keep their idyll secret from the prying eyes of the rest of the world . . . Time alone would tell.

'Morris, why did you never marry?' she asked him one day when they were sitting up in bed after a particularly strenuous bout of love-making, eating their sandwiches. She prepared these each day after breakfast and left them on a tray in the bedroom — nothing wrong with her powers of organisation; she sometimes wondered if a life of deception didn't suit her.

'Why do you want to know?' Simon had his wary look. 'And anyway, how am I supposed to answer? I don't know why I've never married — I haven't, that's all. I do admit to being engaged once.'

'Oh. Who broke it off?'

'She did, of course.'

'Oh.' Bet munched her cold beef sandwich, not knowing what to say. Sometimes he told her things that weren't true, just to see how she would react. However, she had a feeling this was true.

'OK, I'll tell you about it, though why you should want to know beats me; it was years ago and not a particularly edifying story. Caroline was a truly golden girl. We met at university, and for some unknown reason she fell for me. I fell for her, of course, but she could take her pick. We got engaged — much to my family's delight and amazement; hers weren't so delighted, but they made the best of it. Everything was arranged; announcement in *The Times* and all that rubbish, a great big pukka wedding with all the trimmings. Then, to cut a long story short, she turned up unexpectedly at my digs a couple of nights before the wedding and found me in bed with some bird I'd picked up in the local. She just stood there in the doorway, not saying anything. Then she went away. The next day she sent the ring back, her father offered to horsewhip me, the reception at the Hyde Park Hotel was cancelled, the vicar was informed, and that was that. And if

110

you're going to ask the question I see already hovering on your lips — Why was I in bed with a bird I picked up in the local when I was going to marry a gorgeous girl like Caroline? — I can only say I've no idea; it was incredibly bloody stupid, that's all.'

There was a long silence. Then Bet said: 'If it hadn't happened, I mean, if Caroline hadn't found you, d'you think you'd still be married?'

'Gracious me, I've no idea, probably not, but you never know. She was one hell of a girl, and to coin a cliché, a damned sight too good for me.' He yawned and ran his finger down her backbone in the way she loved. 'That's enough of reminiscences, it's time you did some work, you lazy bitch . . . '

Nell was the first to notice a change in her mother and, as was her habit, consulted Bernie. They were driving home from work one Friday. 'Noticed what?' Bernie said, not interested; he was busy planning their visit to a boatyard the following morning. A mate of his from the Life department had said What was the good of living in an area like this and not having a boat? It would revolutionise his life, the mate said, and Bernie had decided to look into it.

'Noticed that Mum's, well, different; sort of dreamy and off-beam. You don't think she's on drugs, do you?'

'Of course she isn't on drugs! You worry too much about your mother, she's perfectly capable of looking after herself. Now, can you be finished by half-ten tomorrow, then we can arrange to meet John at the boatyard at eleven, and that should give us time . . . '

Diz was too immersed in last-minute revising for A-Levels to notice anything much. As always, he'd left revision far too late for comfort, relying on his formidable memory to pull him through. However, even he began to wonder a little about his mother, and went so far as to wake her up one evening when he found her unexpectedly asleep in her armchair at the early hour of nine o'clock, to ask if anything was wrong. 'You do look a bit pale, Mum, and there's that place on your neck. Perhaps you should see the doc, get a tonic or something. We can't have you cracking up while the Duponts are here.'

'Bother the Duponts!'

'There *is* something wrong with you. I knew there was.'

111

But it was Pete who hit the jackpot. It happened one Saturday evening a couple of weeks after the affair with Simon had started, when he popped in to Bet to borrow some ice, the Redford super-de-luxe fridge being once again on the blink. 'Anyone at home?' And as Bet turned round from peeling potatoes at the sink, Pete knew at once — you only had to look at her. He knew too that it must be that chap Morris, it couldn't be anyone else. What a damned shame! Pete wasn't given to thinking serious thoughts, he didn't happen to be made that way, but he was fond of Bet, very fond, and it did seem such a waste that all that integrity and sex appeal should be lavished on someone like Simon Morris. OK, he was jealous, wouldn't at all mind being in Morris's shoes himself, but that was neither here nor there.

'Get me a drink, will you, Pete, while you're at it. We're out of everything but sweet cider and Ron S.'s dandelion wine, and I feel badly in need of a stimulant.' Pete extracted the little cubes of ice from their plastic cases with the expertise born of long practise. 'You don't look in need of a stimulant to me, ducky, quite the reverse. But I'll gladly bring you a drink — a whole bottle, if you like — on one condition.'

'What?'

'That you tell all.'

'All?'

'All.'

And of course she did. Pete was like that. She ended up crying on his shoulder. 'Ducky, please don't cry. I thought you said it was all so wonderful — '

'It is, of course it is. I'm a new woman and all that rubbish, but — '

'You're wondering what's going to happen next. Women always do; they never seem able just to enjoy the moment for its own sake, always have to be thinking ahead. The question is, do you love the guy?'

'Do you love Janice?' Janice was the girl who did the photocopying in Pete's office. Pete, or so he had told Bet, had been crazy about her for months. 'It's not the same thing at all. Anyway, didn't I tell you she's getting married. Some damned Aussi in the next bedsitter; she's going back to Adelaide with him. As a matter of fact the wedding's next week – she's asked me to give her away.'

'And you'll give her a bloody great wedding present too, I don't doubt. Poor old Pete, are you dreadfully upset, you've been so good to her.'

'To tell you the truth, there's this new girl in the typing pool, started a few weeks ago. She did a job for me the other day and we got talking – you know how it is.' Bet nodded, she knew how it was with Pete anyway, and God knew, she wished that was how it was with her. 'What's her name?'

'Karen. Mother's Danish. She's tall and blonde and her legs ...' He became aware that they'd somehow drifted away from the subject in hand. 'That's enough of that, you're the one on the agenda, not your poor old Uncle Pete. Now look, ducky, I know you get cross if anyone mentions the chap's track record, but honestly, for your own sake, you must bear it in mind. No one wants you to be hurt, you've had enough pain, God knows.' He took her chin in his hand and pulled her face towards his. 'You don't want to marry him, do you?'

'Marry him? Of course not. I simply want ...' And she was just trying to work out what it was that she did want when Pol, who appeared to have been eavesdropping outside in the yard, stuck her head through the window. 'So there you are, Pete, I might have known! I asked you to keep an eye on the soufflé while I was in the bath – it's completely ruined. Do I always have to do everything myself?'

This was altogether too much. Bet, taken off balance, lost her temper. Experiencing an overwhelming urge to knock her sister off her self-constructed pedestal, and throwing caution to the winds, she let rip. Pol listened – she couldn't do anything else – her mouth opening and shutting like a fish, two red spots of anger blossoming on her cheeks. Was she going to burst into tears? Feeling savage and guilty at the same time, Bet hoped so. But Pol didn't cry, she was made of sterner stuff. Arms akimbo, eyes flashing, blonde hair blowing in the evening breeze, she stuck it out; then, when at last Bet's powers of invective finally ran out, she too let rip.

'I can only assume,' she shouted back in a clear, carrying voice as crammed with disdain as she could make it, 'that you've been drinking again, Bet. One would have thought you were old enough by now to accept too much alcohol doesn't agree with you, as I'm sure Pete — Pete, unheeded, moaned a disclaimer — 'and Miles if he were here, would agree. But then of course you never learn, do you. The fact that I have a husband and you don't is hardly my fault, and certainly no reason for you to hurl childish abuse at me, as I'm sure you will be the first to admit when you've managed to sober up a bit — '

'Watch it!' Too late, an anguished shout of warning from Pete. Bet had already seized a potato — the large one full of eyes — and hurled it through the window at her sister. It hit Pol slap in the middle of her chest, bounced off and dropped on the flowerbed, leaving a muddy trail of water all down Pol's brand new Harvey & Nichols pink cotton shirt-waister.

Suddenly the years fled away, Pete was forgotten, and the sisters were back in the nursery fighting over the rocking-horse — He's mine! He isn't, Mum said we'd got to share him! No she didn't, she said I was in charge and you had to ask me first if you wanted to ride him! She didn't, you know she didn't, you rotten little bully! Quick as a flash, Pol bent down and retrieved the potato, took aim — she hadn't been fast bowler in the school first eleven for nothing — and bowled it back through the window. Bet, always quicker on the uptake than her sister, leaped nimbly out of its path, and the potato, knocking Pete's glass out of his hand on the way, landed with a crash against the kitchen dresses, breaking two dinner plates, a glass water jug and a hideous china windmill Diz had once brought back from a school trip to Holland. Pausing only for a second to survey with considerable satis-faction the damage she'd done, Pol legged it through the gate into the kitchen garden, back to the comparative safety of her end of the house.

'Just make sure your wife never crosses this threshold again, Pete, will you,' panted Bet, bosom heaving, a knife from the draining-board in her hand, 'because if she does, I won't be answerable for the consequences.' Then she too fled, leaving Pete alone and near to tears, to clear up the mess.

When Simon heard the story on Monday afternoon he laughed till he cried. Bet crossly threw the soap at him. They'd taken to having baths together now, an idea quite novel to Bet. She and Miles had never shared a bath, he'd been too big for the two of them to fit comfortably into one, besides, he preferred a shower. 'It's not that funny. You've absolutely no idea what my sister can be like. I often wonder how Pete's managed to put up with her all these years, he must be some kind of a saint.'

'Long-suffering, yes, but not, one would have thought, quite the stuff of saints; more some kind of idiot. Turn on the hot tap, darling, there's a good girl, it's getting cold my end. So what happens now?'

'Oh, I expect it'll blow over. But she'll damn well stump up for those plates.'

'Scrooge! What about that caviar and all those drinks?'

'Shut up, shut up, or I'll drown you, you randy little wop!' Bet leapt on him, pressing his head down into the water. A large pool began to form on the bathroom floor, and after a time the water started gently to drip through the ceiling of Nell and Bernie's sitting-room.

'Mum is *up* to something — I told you.' Nell and Bernie stood looking up at the damp patch on their ceiling. 'Nonsense, she just let the bath run over, that's all. Perhaps she fell asleep, you said she's been looking tired lately.'

'But Mum never has a bath in the daytime.'

'So people change their habits.'

'Something's going on, I know it is. Why, for instance, does she never mention Simon Morris? They were as thick as thieves at the party, and he told me he would be staying at the Manor while Miss Westover's away. What's more, I bumped into Mrs Bone in town yesterday, and she said Simon was here one afternoon last week; she happened to be passing in the bus and saw his car parked in our yard. How come Mum never mentioned it?'

'And you think your Mum and Simon Morris are having baths together in the afternoons?' Bernie said, meaning it as a joke, then suddenly thinking it might not be.

'It's possible, I suppose ... but Mum ... Surely she wouldn't, not Mum ...?'

They looked at each other.

'You know Bet's having baths with that man now?'

Pete choked over his drink. 'Baths, ducky?' Good Lord,

was she now. 'Yes, baths. They let the water run over and ruined poor Nelly's sitting-room ceiling; Bernie's only just finished decorating, too.'

'Bad show. I mean, about the ceiling. But I don't see how the blame can be laid at poor old Morris's door. How do Nell and Bernie know?'

'Someone saw his car parked in the yard, and apparently it's there every afternoon, so of course the whole village knows by now what's going on.'

'But what about the bath? I still don't see — '

'It would be perfectly obvious to anyone but you. Nell says the bathroom was completely flooded and a whole bottle of that Arden stuff I gave her for Christmas had been used up, and Bernie said the place stank like a brothel. Apparently all Bet could come up with was that she must have gone out and left the bathroom tap on.'

'Just out of interest, how does Bernie know what a brothel smells like?'

'Don't try and change the subject. In my opinion you know far more about the whole business than you pretend. Bet's told you, hasn't she, she's told you she's having an affair with Simon Morris?'

So the old girl hadn't overheard his and Bet's conversation in the kitchen after all, one must be thankful for small mercies. 'Oh all right then, she has. And good luck to her, I say. I'm only sorry she's fallen for a chap like that, because quite frankly I can't see any good coming out of it.'

'Are you saying you condone Bet's behaviour? A woman of her age, carrying on like a love-sick teenager, flaunting her lover — a man like that, with a notorious reputation — in front of the entire village? Flooding her own daughter's sitting-room, drinking, fornicating . . .'

Pete waited quietly for her to run out of steam. When she had, he said gently, as one speaking to a child: 'You do know you're talking the most utter balls, ducky, don't you?'

Pol sniffed. A small tear began to roll down her cheek. Pete knelt beside her, a whale amongst the fashionable Victoriana in their tiny Chelsea drawing-room. She sniffed again and buried her face in his shoulder. 'It's that stupid row you and Bet had, isn't it?' Pol nodded her head two or three times.

116

Pete stroked her hair. 'Bet's a damned attractive woman still, ducky. She had a hell of a shock when old Miles died. This was bound to happen sooner or later — something had to give.' Pol looked at him, her face vulnerable for once; that look Pete knew well, it was the look that had caused him to fall in love with her in the first place.

'But Pete, to go overboard with Simon Morris of all people. He'll ditch her just as soon as he finds someone more interesting, you know he will. And I know you think I'm stupid and old-fashioned, but it's not a good thing for the rest of us if Bet gets a name in the village for behaving oddly. Imagine what poor Bernie must feel, with his mother-in-law carrying on like that.'

'Bernie'll get by, it's Bet I'm worried about. The snag is, she really does seem to have gone a bit over the top for the damned chap.'

Pol sat up and tidied her face in the mirror opposite; Second Empire cherubs danced lewdly round its rim but she ignored them. 'We'll have to find her someone else, that's all.'

Pete looked at her in admiration. 'But shall we be able to?'

'We can but try.'

Later that evening, after a cosy dinner *en famille*, Pete, waking from his post-dinner nap, got up from his chair and switched off the television. 'Ducky?'

'Yes.'

'You know Bet and that Morris chap.'

'Yes?'

'They've given me an idea. Why don't we do what they did?'

Pol's neatly plucked brows shot up in shocked surprise. 'Do what they did?'

'I mean, why don't we have a bath together; it might be fun. We could put some of that bubble stuff in it, and there's plenty of room for the two of us in that new Italian job you insisted on buying. And Pol?'

'??'

'Bags I the tap end.'

117

Chapter Eleven

'The train now approaching platform two is the thirteen twenty-seven for Liverpool Street only.' Bet, jittery as a maybug, clutching an overnight bag and far too hot in a denim trouser suit, stood alone on a packed platform at Stourwick station, about to embark on a weekend with Simon Morris. The weekend was bound to be a disaster, it couldn't be anything else, but like the stock figure in a Greek tragedy, Bet felt compelled to go on and meet her doom. Why she seemed unable to look forward to the weekend like a normal person, she simply didn't know. What was wrong with a couple of nights in London with an attractive man when you were both unattached, for God's sake?

The train roared in, stinking of diesel, and there was no time to think any more; Bet was on it, and the die was cast. She found a seat, sat down and tried to relax. She must stop wondering what was going on at home, forget the sweat trickling down her back, and above all try not to speculate on why Simon had asked her to London in the first place.

It was early June now, and she hadn't seen him since their three weeks' idyll had officially come to an end just over a fortnight ago. It had been absolutely splendid, Simon said, not looking at her; he'd not enjoyed anything so much for years, and it only went to show what fun things can be if both of you are uncommitted. 'Yes, doesn't it?' Bet said, engulfed in misery and cursing the still, small voice inside her that kept repeating 'I told you so'. But at least he had invited her to dine at the Manor for a farewell celebration. 'The food won't be up to much, Alfonso and I aren't on speaking terms, but I can vouch for the wine.'

Initially, the dinner was a success, in spite of the food. Alfonso having made a last-minute decision to take the evening off, the fare consisted of a slice or two of what used to be known as Spam, a limp lettuce, and one of Mr Kipling's fruit pies; the wine, however, was all it had been cracked up to be. They'd dined in a shabby, doggy room known as the morning-room, opening on to a conservatory. 'Sorry about the smell of dog,' Simon said, 'but one gets used to it. It still upsets Alfonso, but then I don't think Spaniards like dogs much.'

The conservatory was lovely, and in contrast to the morning-room, smelt of lemon verbena and honey. It was littered with basket chairs, battered sofas, old geraniums and back numbers of *Horse and Hound*. At the far end, bunches of tiny, hard, green grapes hung down like Chinese lanterns from the tentacles of a surprisingly luxuriant vine. Outside, in the middle of a small, weedy lawn badly in need of cutting, danced a broken statue of Eros. He'd always loved this part of the house, Simon said, ever since he was a child. They'd had wonderful games here, he and Cyn, and in those days there'd been a grass tennis court beyond the box hedge that bordered the lawn.

It was while they were drinking their after-dinner coffee — Nescafé in Spode cups — that Bet asked Simon about his father. She'd never dared before, but somehow now it no longer seemed to matter. 'My dad?' Simon took a gulp of coffee, grimaced, and gave the patiently waiting marmalade dog a lump of sugar. 'Hasn't Christine Barnet told you all? I believe the legend goes he was an Italian piano tuner; I've even heard it mooted that he was an organ grinder, though how that particular story got off the ground I'll never know.

'He was, however, Italian. He came over here in the summer of thirty-nine to value and restore some of the furniture. My grandmother suddenly decided something should be done about it and my great-uncle Arthur, who happened to be in antiques, produced my dad. That's what my dad did, you see. He spent his summers staying in the houses of the rich, advising them on their possessions and

119

occasionally doing a little modest restoration work, and his winters rather more uncomfortably in a bedsitter in Milan, writing not very good articles for various periodicals, and chatting up rich women. Anyway, my mum, a galumphing eighteen-year-old at the time, who'd never been known before to show the slightest enthusiasm for anything other than a horse, fell madly in love with him, and somehow persuaded the poor chap to run off with her.

'Of course there was an appalling family row, which reached epic proportions when it was revealed after they'd gone that not only had dad seduced mother − actually I've always had my doubts about this and wouldn't mind betting it was mother who did the seducing; we Westovers are a determined lot and mother's a pretty big woman to boot − but half the girls in the village as well. However, when it was discovered that the worst had happened and mother was in pup, my grandparents relented, and on a downpayment of five hundred pounds the truants were married at a register office in London, three weeks before the outbreak of World War Two.

'Not long after that my dad returned to Italy, where he joined the army and subsequently − no doubt to the relief of all concerned − got himself killed early in forty-three. I don't think mother ever heard from him after he went back to Italy; she was simply notified of his death by the War Office. I appeared just as the phony war was coming to an end, and as the last thing Mother wanted was a baby around, spolling her fun, I was shipped down here and virtually adopted by my grandparents, leaving Mother to enjoy her war in peace.

'Running away with my dad was the only original thing Mother ever did. After the war she married my stepfather, a monumental bore by the name of Reggie Morris, and bought a riding school near Camberley. They live there to this day. I pay them an annual visit − God knows why, some sort of misplaced sense of filial duty, I suppose − when Mother keeps me up to date with the latest news on her horses, wonders why I never married, and complains incessantly about the ills inherent in the permissive society. Old Cyn has her faults, she's rude and philistine and drinks too much, but she does live and let live, and I've always loved this place.'

120

'Do you know what your father looked like?' Bet, fascinated, saw it all. The galumphing, privileged girl in her jodhpurs and Aertex shirt that last, baking summer before the war. Hitler's armies on the march, marionette figures with arms raised in the Nazi salute, strutting through country after beaten country, pursued by rumbling tanks. Evacuees, gas masks, Peace in our Time, strawberries for tea, village cricket, gymkhanas. The young, dark-haired, doomed Italian, exotic as a peacock in a farmyard; like Simon, only not like Simon ...' Kiss me, Angelo ... I love you, love you, love you ... Better than the horses, better than Daddy and Mummy, better than anything ...'

'Are you listening, Titania, you've a faraway look in your eye. Yes, I do know what he looked like, I've a photo of him somewhere, one of those sepia affairs taken in the twenties. He looks like a poor man's Rudolf Valentino − hair smarmed down and parted in the middle, a stiff collar, and believe it not, carrying a prayer book.'

'Oh.' Bet, for once, could think of nothing to say. Simon got up and poured himself another brandy. 'Come on, there's no need to look so serious. I've been damned lucky, you know, and the last thing I had was a deprived childhood; any buggering up of my life has been done strictly by myself alone.' He bent down and kissed the back of her neck. 'Enough of this soul-searching, haven't we some unfinished business to attend to?' They made love then, on one of the broken-down sofas, in the depths of which Simon found an old marrow bone.

Bet closed her eyes as the train rushed through Chelmsford and saw again the brown moths flying about the guttering candles on the dinner table, smelt the scent of lemon verbena, tasted the salt of her own tears. It had not been the same as before, their love-making, she'd felt too sad, her thoughts continually drifting forward to the time when Simon would be gone from her. Indeed, after a bit he'd sat up, shaking the fluff and dust from the sofa out of his hair and saying crossly: 'We don't seem to be getting anywhere much with this, do we? Perhaps it's time I took you home.' Of course she apologised, tried to explain, but it wasn't any good, he either couldn't or wouldn't understand.

121

Then, to crown it all, they had a row. The first they'd ever had. 'Look, Titania, I don't want to hurry you, but can you start collecting your things, I have to be back here by ten forty-five, Cyn's ringing from the States.' And that had really riled her. 'For Christ's sake! If it's that much bother I'll ring Bernie and get him to collect me.'

'Oh, don't be childish, if it's anything I hate it's childish women. Of course I'll drive you home, but I have to be back by ten forty-five, that's all — I promised Cyn. It's to do with a deal she's involved in over there, and it's important.'

After that they hadn't spoken until he dropped her at the Rectory gate.

'Goodnight, Simon, thank you for the dinner.'

'Come on, Titania, no need to sulk, you're a big girl now, you know.' Then he'd kissed her on the top of her head, squeezed her hand, and driven off into the night.

A few days after that — days plodded through somehow, cooking, gardening, walking Tib, listening to Christine's gossip, arguing with Diz — Nell, jubilant, had announced that she was pregnant, the baby due in December. They celebrated her news with dinner at The George, and for a few short hours, in the excitement of hearing she was to become a grandmother, Bet forgot Simon. But the euphoria was short-lived. Nell began to suffer from morning sickness; not only morning sickness, either; almost every type of food appeared to disagree with her. Bet who had never suffered a moment's discomfort with either of her pregnancies, found her sympathy wearing a little thin, and burst into tears of frustration and longing when forced one evening to rush into the garden with a pan of gently frying onions, pursued by despairing wails of, 'Oh please, Mum, *not* onions!'

Then, when she had finally convinced herself that their abortive evening at the Manor had been her last with Simon, he rang. What was more — so typical of a man! — he chose the one moment when she would have been quite happy if he hadn't. It was the night of the Redford dinner party, she and Pol by this time having made it up; an uncharacteristic aspect of their reconciliation this time was that Pol had been the first to offer the olive branch; usually it was the other way round, with Pol frightened of a rebuff, hanging about looking miserable, and waiting for Bet to make the first move. The dinner party consisted of the Redfords, the Cornwalls, and a friend of theirs as a token man for Bet. The token man, as it happened, turned out to be surprisingly nice. Small (but most men seemed on the small side after Miles), glasses (so what?), with a marked resemblance to a very intelligent-looking fox terrier (she loved dogs, didn't she?) But definitely nice, and what was more, funny with it. Pol introduced him with all the smugness of a conjuror producing a rabbit from his hat: 'Bet, dear, this is Donald Stewart. Donald's an archaeologist, he's written a lot of books and he knew Miles at Cambridge.'

And there he was, a jolly, sandy-haired man looking rather sheepish. 'Look, you probably hate archaeology and loathe meeting old university chums of your husband's. If so, do please say so and I promise to leave you in peace. Alternatively, I have one or two other topics of conversation up my sleeve. While you're making up your mind, why not have a peanut?'

Suddenly, absurdly, she'd felt like an orphan brought in from the storm. She'd accepted the peanut, said that on the contrary, she was interested in archaeology and she did like meeting old friends of Miles, and where was his wife? He said his wife had run off with a skiing instructor years ago, and would Bet like to come to tea at his place in the not too distant future? He possessed, he went on to say, quite a reasonable collection of Bronze Age pots, but if these failed to please there were always the roses, and his daily was an absolute dab hand at making scones. Bet said yes, she'd love to, and it went on from there.'

It were therefore rather irritating that on her return to her part of the house, feeling happier than she had for months, she was greeted by Nell with the news that Simon had rung. 'He said he'd ring back later, but I wouldn't bank on it.'

She didn't, and stoically made ready for bed. However, as usual taking her by surprise, he did ring back — just as she was drifting into an uneasy doze. 'I rang earlier and you were out.' He sounded aggrieved.

'Pol had a dinner party.'

'Oh. Anyone interesting?'

'An archaeologist who likes dogs. His wife ran off with a skiing instructor.'

'I see. In that case you probably won't be interested in my proposition.'

'Proposition?' God, what now?

'Do you want to come to London next weekend?'

'London?'

'Yes, London. And must you keep repeating everything I say?'

'It would be nice, but . . .'

'You'll have to make your mind up fairly quickly, Johnny Backhouse needs to know by Monday.'

'Who is Johnny Backhouse, and what's he got to do with it?'

'He's offered me his flat in Chelsea, it's a bit on the noisy side, but I haven't a pad of my own at the moment; I'm away so much it's not worth the expense, so I mostly doss down with friends.'

'I see,' she said, playing for time. There was silence while she rubbed one foot against the other. Her feet were freezing; in the excitement of answering the phone she'd forgotten her slippers.

'Have you fallen asleep?' He sounded reproachful now. 'Or perhaps just not keen? The last time we met, I had the distinct impression you would welcome the idea of a weekend together. If I'm wrong, please, do say so.'

'You're not wrong. It's just, well, next weekend is rather soon, and what will I say to everyone'

'I'm sure you'll think of something. Look, I'll ring you on Sunday evening, OK?'

She told them she was spending the weekend in Beaconsfield with Maeve; Dicky was away, Maeve on her own, and it seemed a good opportunity to get together, they'd been meaning to for ages — which was true. Maeve Riley and Bet had been best friends since O-Level days in the upper fifth, and until they married, had told each other everything. After that, things weren't quite the same; they never were, were they, when people married, and Miles and Dicky hadn't got on. But for all that, Maeve was the person Bet felt she could turn to in a crisis of this sort. Come to think of it, hadn't

Maeve herself once gone off the rails? Some mature student of Dicky's who wanted her to run away with him to Bangladesh and work for Oxfam.

In fact, when Bet asked for her alibi — late at night on the phone in a whisper, though why she had to whisper she didn't know, there was no one about to hear her — Maeve sounded quite excited. 'How splendid, Bet, but why the secrecy? I mean, he isn't married, is he?'

Why indeed? Bet's mind slid away from the problem. 'No, he's not married.'

'A flat in Chelsea, I'm green with envy. But what about Pol?'

'Off to St Andrew's for the weekend. And may I give you the number of the flat when I know it, just in case?'

'OK, darling. I mean, what are friends for? But I'll want a full report. By the way, can I tell Dicky?'

'Would you mind awfully not, I feel such a fool . . .'

'Tickets please.' Bet sat up; Bethnal Green already, they were almost there.

'A bit on the sticky side, isn't it — can I help you down with your case?' The elderly man seated opposite looked her up and down, and smiled ingratiatingly.

'Thank you, I'm sure I can manage.'

'Nonsense, my dear, it's much too heavy.' The man smiled harder than ever, and added a wink for good measure. Oh God! It started to rain as she fled down the platform.

Her great adventure had begun.

'This right then, love?' the cab driver asked doubtfully as, twenty minutes later, they pulled up outside a trendy mens' boutique at the wrong end of the Kings Road. The rain sheeted down, and a particularly vivide flash of lightning illuminated the shop front just as Bet was getting out of the taxi.

'It must be, it's the right address.' As a rendezvous for a romantic assignation it couldn't look worse if it tried. Never mind, perhaps it was better inside. 'The entrance must be round the corner, through that door.'

'That'll be it, love, but mind how you go.' The cab drove away, leaving Bet alone in the rain. A tall, grim-faced girl with pink hair opened the pink front door. 'Yeah?'

'Simon Morris? He's borrowed Mr Backhouse's flat . . .'

'Sim's in the bath — you can go up, he won't be long.'

The stairs were steep, and Bet, scattering rain drops, was painfully aware of the sullen girl trudging up behind her. Who on earth was she? Safer not to wonder — never ask questions when you don't want to know the answer, Miles always said. At the top was a small landing smelling of gas and garlic, from which several doors led off. One door, leading into about the most untidy room Bet had ever seen — even Diz in his worst phase had never reached these heights — stood open. 'Make yourself at home,' the girl waved a lethargic arm, 'I'll tell Sim you're here. Coffee?'

'Er . . . thanks.'

The girl disappeared, leaving Bet standing in the middle of the room with her overnight bag at her feet. She was shamefully near to tears, and wondered what to do next. Should she walk out, scream, or just do as she was told — ie make herself at home. But how could anyone but a raving maniac make herself at home in all this racket? Simon's description of the Backhouse flat as 'a bit on the noisy side' must be the understatement of the century. What with rain lashing the windows, the roar of traffic outside in the Kings Road and the gibbering of a television crouched malevolently in the far corner, you couldn't hear yourself think, let alone make yourself at home.

'Sorry, we're out of milk — black do you?' The girl was back again, this time with a brimming mug of treacly coffee. 'Fine . . . er . . . I wonder, do you think we might turn the TV down a bit?'

'Sim wants it for the racing,' the girl said, and disappeared again. Bet, seething, threw herself down on the nearest armchair, then discovered she'd sat on a bag of doughnuts.

'Hullo, darling, be with you in a minute.' Simon stood there, fresh from his bath, hair wet, a towel draped round his middle. 'Simon, I've sat on a bag of doughnuts, and unless you turn that bloody noise off, I'm going . . .'

The pink-haired girl, whose name turned out to be Bo, left at last, taking with her the bag of doughnuts and a sack of washing, and they made love on Johnny Backhouse's bed to the accompaniment of the rush hour traffic and rock music from the flat upstairs.

126

'Who actually is Bo?' she asked.

'No one, really. Just a friend.'

'Does she always talk in monosyllables'

'Most of the time, but she's a good sort.'

'Will she be coming back with the washing soon?'

'Not while you're here.'

But then nothing was as it should have been.

Before they went to bed properly, Bet tried to tidy up the flat a bit, but Simon said to leave it alone. Never to tidy the place was, he said, the only stipulation Johnny Backhouse made to his weekend tenants; he wouldn't know where anything was if they did. Quite sensible when you came to think about it. Bet nodded wearily. She began to worry about Tib; had Diz remembered to take him for his walk?

The following afternoon Bet and Simon went on a boat down the river to Greenwich. Although it wasn't sunny, the rain had stopped and it was quite warm. They sat in the stern, holding hands and giggling at the guide's patter. A fat American lady took a picture of Simon, the outline of dockland behind him. 'It always helps to have a figure in a landscape,' she said, 'and Hiram's none too photogenic.' Later, they sat in a dusty tea-shop in Greenwich eating sticky cakes and, briefly, life was fun, Bo and the ghastly flat forgotten.

'I think I'll go back today, after all.' It was Sunday; the bells of St Luke's church, Chelsea, were ringing for morning service, and Bet and Simon were the only customers in Colonel Foster's Chicken Parlour. 'But Simon,' she'd said, 'after last night I don't think I could cope with chicken for breakfast.' 'Don't be an ass, we can have coffee and rolls, can't we?' But the coffee turned out to be half-cold, the rolls tasted of rubber, and the stale smell of last night's chicken filled the air. The waitress looked at them sourly; the place was open, but she hadn't bargained for customers yet. She put on a tape; that should get rid of them, they didn't look the sort who'd like music first thing, it was a mystery to her what they were doing here anyway. But she hadn't bargained for Simon who, with a hint of Westover authority in his voice, commanded her to 'switch that damned thing off' − which, taken by surprise and eyeing him with respect, she did. Quite dishy really, she decided, but a bit on the old side.

Simon lit a cigarette. 'This weekend hasn't been a frightful success, has it?' Bet looked at her plate. 'Not really.'

'Not a lot we can do about it, is there?' He took her hand and kissed it. All sorts of things they could do about it flashed through Bet's mind, each one discarded as soon as it showed its face. She stirred her lacklustre coffee. 'Are you saying this is it, then?'

'I'm not saying anything of the kind! Why do women always have to be so literal?' Did she detect a slightly querulous note in his voice? She pressed on. 'I don't happen to be 'women', I happen to be me. And I'm not being literal, whatever that means. It just seems to me that what you want is to have your cake and eat it.' He looked up then and smiled. She wished that smile didn't still make her heart turn over, but it did.

'I'm not alone in that, for God's sake! Most people would like to if they thought they could get away with it.'

'Look, Simon, I'm being serious. It's no use playing games with me, I don't know the rules and it's far too late in the day for me to learn. Let's face it, this weekend's been a disaster. I can't and won't put up with the likes of Bo and I'm not cut out for *la vie Bohème*, and there it is. If that's what you want, then —'

'I told you — Bo's just a girl.'

'Aren't they all?'

'Look, Titania, I'm sorry but I'm not up to serious conversations at this hour of the morning. In any case, soul-baring has never been much in my line. If two people are reduced to discussing their relationship, then in my opinion that relationship's a dead duck and not worth the bother anyway. Just because you didn't go a bundle on poor old Backhouses's flat, and Bo happened to turn up to collect my washing, it isn't the end of the world, or for that matter —'

'The end of the affair?' Bet was near to tears; her eyes were smarting from lack of sleep, and she had a lump in her throat the size of a hen's egg. There was a long silence while Simon frowned down at the bill, then feeling in his pockets for change, made the discovery that he hadn't any. 'Look, Bet, I know you'll think I'm trying to get off the subject, but there seems to be a bit of a crisis on. Like the ass I am, I appear to have left all my money in the flat, you don't think you could possibly oblige ...?'

'Oh God, Simon, you're so ... so utterly hopeless!' But she was giggling all the same as she opened her bag. 'How much?'

'More than it bloody should be. Just give me your purse.' Hand outstretched, he grinned across the table at her, a small boy let off being sent to bed without his supper. 'You're a remarkable girl, Bet Brandon, and don't let anyone tell you otherwise.' He took the proffered purse and jumped briskly to his feet. 'Now, as we still have a couple of hours before you leave for your train, what d'you suggest we do? I know what I'd like to do, but it's your treat, so ...?'

Bet looked at him helplessly, she felt like someone drowning in glue. 'If it's what I think it is, I have to admit that it's what I should like to do too, so we might as well do it, mightn't we?'

They said goodbye in Johnny Backhouse's awful flat. He wouldn't come to the station with her, Simon said, he'd always hated saying goodbye at stations, it reminded him of going back to school. 'But, joking apart, it has been fun, Titania, surely you will admit that? Not this weekend perhaps, I realise that's been a bit of a flop, but all the other times?' He sounded like a hospital visitor trying to cheer up a sick relative. Bet nodded sadly, knowing now that she wasn't cut out to be a hedonist after all. And if feeling the way she did was the price one had to pay for fun − or Simon's particular brand of fun, anyway − quite frankly, it wasn't worth it.

'It is over then, is it?' she said, trying to think straight but not being able to. 'If so, I − ' But it was no good, she couldn't say any more because he was kissing her. And after that the taxi arrived, and after that there was nothing but goodbye left to say.

So ended Bet Brandon's first, and probably last, 'naughty' weekend in London.

'Lunch at the Pigeon Loft, ducky?' Pete turned the car into the Kings Road. The Redfords had caught an early plane back from Scotland; like Bet's, their weekend had not been a success. It had poured with rain from the moment they arrived at St Andrew's to the moment they left it. 'I suppose so,' Pol said, 'there's nothing in the house, and if I don't have something to eat soon I shall pass out from sheer exhaustion.'

There was a sudden screech of brakes and a volley of abuse from the man in the car behind. 'Pete, what on earth ...? Have you taken leave of your senses?' But Pete was looking after a retreating taxi. 'Do you know, I could have sworn it was Bet in that taxi.'

'Bet? But she's in Beaconsfield.'

Pete smiled. 'I don't think she is.'

'Make up your bloody mind, mate.' The man in the car behind pressed his horn hard down. 'Some of us have work to do.'

'Nelly dear, how are you? ... No, dear, we came back early, it poured with rain the whole time. Then Sally Monroe started flu and Jack said they'd better get back before it got any worse, so Pete and I thought there wasn't much point in sitting there watching the rain ... I was just ringing to say we'll be down next weekend, and then of course we'll be down for ten days ... It's chips now, is it, dear. Well, as I'm sure I've told you, such things do you no good. I never allow Pete any, although he loves them − he's always had such plebian tastes ...

'I must go now, dear, but before I do there is one tiny thing. Be a little careful what you say to your mother when she gets back from her weekend ... No, dear, I think you'll find she gets back today, Pete and I have just seen her in a taxi in the Kings Road ...

'Yes, odd, isn't it. Quite a way from Beaconsfield ...!

'I leave that to your imagination, dear, but I'm sure you're just as capable of putting two and two together as I am. I can only suppose she feels a bit silly. I mean, lets face it, in another few months she'll be a grandmother ... Look, I really must go, dear, Pete wants to watch Greer Garson on the box and I must admit I wouldn't mind seeing her myself. There's not enough good, clean romance any more. I know you all laugh at Barbara Cartland, but personally I think she has a lot going for her ...'

130

Nell replaced the receiver. 'You know what Mum's been up to now?'

'I can't wait to hear,' said Bernie, just managing to tear himself away from his *Reader's Digest*.

'She didn't go to Aunty Maeve's at all, she went to London to spend the weekend with Simon Morris.'

'Good for your Mum! I bet that discovery's made your Aunt Pol's weekend.'

This was obviously one of Bernie's 'difficult' days. Nell sniffed, her eyes beginning to fill with angry tears. 'If you're going to be like that, I'm going for a walk.'

'You do that.' Surely she wasn't going to start crying again? Who wants a family anyway? Bernie, with a sigh of relief, returned to his *Reader's Digest*.

Chapter Twelve

'Mum', said Diz, 'I've just been looking at this recipe in the colour supplement, it looks quite simple really and — '

'Since when have you been interested in cooking?' Bet was wading through the Sunday lunch washing-up, Nell having had to retire to bed in a hurry at the sight of the rhubarb crumble. Light dawned. 'It's those damned Duponts again, isn't it. You think my cooking won't be up to scratch. Let me tell you, good English cooking is all the rage in France; they have English pubs, and fish and chips, and — '

'Who's talking about good English cooking?'

'Get out of here, you little toad, and take your recipe with you. If the Duponts don't like what's given them, they know what they can do.'

At that moment the phone rang. 'It's for you, Mum, the man Morris.'

'Hullo,' she said.

'I can't talk for long,' he said — there seemed an awful lot of background noise — 'I'm at a party.'

'But it's three o'clock in the afternoon.'

'Is it really? The party must have gone on longer than I thought.'

'How's Bo?'

'All right.'

'Are you drunk?'

'Yes.'

'Oh.' Pause. More background noise. 'Just thought I'd ring,' he said, 'to see how you were getting on.'

'All right, I suppose,' she said, 'slaving away as usual.

132

These wretched French friends of Diz arrive tomorrow expecting haute cuisine.'

'Will they get it?'

'No.' She heard him laugh, then an indistinct female voice and the sound of a scuffle. 'Can't talk any longer, the natives are getting restless.'

'OK then, goodbye.' Why did he have to ring at all? She became aware of Diz at her elbow. 'Were you listening?'

'I couldn't help it, could I? Morris sounded a bit pissed to me.'

'Don't be absurd, and don't use that expression, you know I don't like it.'

Back at the washing-up, a tear trickled down Bet's nose into the greasy water, shortly followed by another. Damn and blast the man! What the hell was the point of ringing her up? Surely not just to let her know he was having a ball at some idiotic party. Or had he hoped to make her jealous? Either way, she wished he would leave her alone. She was beginning to feel rather desperate, and if something remotely positive – good or bad, she was past caring which – didn't happen soon, she'd go clean round the bend. All that stupid weekend in London had done was to confirm what she knew already, namely, that she and Simon were simply not cut out for each other – except perhaps in bed, and how long could that last? That he was fond of her she now had no doubt, and she was fond of him – much too fond; but to believe he would be prepared to change his way of life for her was simply pie-in-the-sky, romantic nonsense.

'It's no use, ducky,' Pete had said – thank God for Pete – 'he's not your sort.'

'But how,' she'd asked, feeling rebellious, 'do you – or I, for that matter – know what my sort is? Just because I was married to one type of man doesn't mean that's the only type of man for me.'

'No, ducky, that's not what I meant. Now, if it were that chap Don Stewart.'

'What's he got to do with it?'

'Now, don't bristle up. Went to tea with him didn't you?'

'Yes, I went to tea with him, and a very nice tea we had. I

like Don Stewart and I'm sure he's a first-class archaeologist, but — '

'Don't play the innocent with me, ducky. You're a highly fanciable woman as well you know . . . '

But Bet, scrubbing away at the gravy saucepan with a scourer that should have been thrown out weeks ago, wondered whether she really was. OK, men like that man on the train and Ron Stokes fancied her, but sex to them was surely just a biological urge; like a dog pursuing a bitch on heat. In the end, whichever way one looked at it, it all boiled down to the same old well-tried cliché; a woman wanted a lover, a man wanted sex. Not that she didn't want sex, far from it, but she wanted all sorts of other things to go with it. Whereas Simon . . . well, all Simon appeared to want was to mess around with pink-haired morons half his age and names like Bo. And if the whole thing wasn't so bloody miserable it would be farcical — no doubt others already saw it that way. And perhaps, like the real Titania, she really had been bewitched. Or perhaps, and more likely, things up to now had been too easy, and the Fates in their wisdom had decided that the time had come for her to pay.

Having finished the washing-up at last, she decided to go upstairs and inspect the Dupont sleeping arrangements; it might, if nothing else, take her mind off things. Jean-Pierre was to share with Diz, and Liza to have the tiny room over the porch. Liza's room was only just big enough for a bed and dressing-table, but nevertheless looked quite pretty. A young girl's bedroom; soft pink walls, curtains and bedspread to match. She must remember to pick some roses in the morning for a vase on the dressing-table; some of those pale pink climbers behind the garage, with the heavenly scent — young girls liked that sort of thing. She sat down on the bed and closed her eyes. At least the next few weeks should be so busy that she would have little time to think: Diz at home, the Duponts, Pol and Pete down for ten days. Then, of course, there was the bloody village fête.

How could she have been so idiotic as to promise Mrs Snately the Rectory garden for it? But she had, and that was that. She could hardly go back on her promise now. At least — and Bet would never know how her sister had achieved such a coup, or indeed whether Angie Snately was pleased or appalled by the development — Pol had taken over the running of the fête. And, naturally, Pol was in her element. Not since that last, halcyon term at St Christopher's when she was head girl had she enjoyed herself so much. Committees proliferated under her hand, coffee parties bourgeoned, friendships blossomed. Smiling ladies ran hither and thither at her command, only too eager, it seemed, to oblige her every whim. It was all, they told Bet as they dashed about laden with home-made teddies, perfectly knitted matinée jackets and lists for the white elephant stall, turning out to be such fun. Mrs Redford was such a good sort, wasn't she, and such a change from old Ma Snately. Bet's role in all this — one had to be thankful for small mercies — was that of humble tea-maker, and she would do a possible two-hour stint on the cake stall. 'That is,' Pol had said nastily the other evening on the phone (if people only knew what she was really like), 'if you can spare the time from your other activities . . .'

'Now, Mum, can we go over the programme just once more. We have the daube for supper tonight, OK? Plus salad and Sid Kettle's strawberries for afters, plus those two bottles of wine I won in the Co-op raffle. Then Nell and Bern, having already eaten, join us for coffee, then —'

'Count me out for coffee.' Bernie, in a track suit, closed his eyes wearily. 'I've work to do this evening.'

The three of them, Bet, Diz and Bernie, stood shivering in the booking hall at Stourwick station, waiting for the Duponts' train, the day as cold as only an English June day can be. Bernie opened his eyes and went into his running-on-the spot routine. 'I hope the train isn't late, I really do have a lot on. Didn't you say the sister can drive?'

'Yes, she's frightfully good, all the French are.'

'If that's the case, why not hire a self-drive for the week, then the three of you can go round together.'

'The train arriving at platform three is the seventeen forty-five from Liverpool Street to Norwich, stopping at . . .'

'They're here! Come on, Mum, we must be there to welcome them, it looks so bad if no one's around.' Diz thrust himself into the crowd, Bet and Bernie trailing after him.

'Dizzy, Dizzy, how are you?' A tall, pleasant-faced youth, hung about with the usual paraphernalia of rucksacks and cameras, burst through the jumble of tired-faced commuters. 'Great JP, great! May I introduce my mother ...' Embraces all round. Bet felt relieved; he didn't look too bad at all. But where was the sister?

Then they saw her.

Tiny, perfect, she was an enchanted figure straight out of the *Arabian Nights*. She had almond eyes and golden skin; she had black hair, its snaky ringlets caught up in a tortoiseshell comb at the side of her head, and perfect breasts swelling gently under her dusty pink bush jacket. She was followed by, of all people, old Monty Cornwall carrying her rucksack.

'Is that ...?' Bernie, with an all too audible gasp, pushed forward to introduce himself before anyone else had a look-in. Bet had never seen him so animated. 'I'm Diz's brother-in-law, Bernie, welcome to England, Liza — is this your first visit?'

''Allo, Bernee. Yes, it is my first visit to the UK. It is always so cold?' One might have known her voice would be as enchanting as the rest of the damned girl; husky, lilting, the accent amusingly pronounced. Bet, her mouth dry, put a brave face on it. 'Hullo, my dear, I'm Diz's mother. How very nice to meet you at last.'

Bernie seemed, quite literally, to have taken leave of his senses. He took no steps whatsoever to conceal his admiration for Liza, and throughout the car journey home did all he could to monopolise her attention. On their arrival at the Rectory, he added insult to injury by hovering solicitously in the doorway while Bet showed Liza her bedroom; Bet was sure he would have accompanied her to the loo if she had not forcibly restrained him. Nell, needless to say, took exception to all this, and instead of behaving like a sensible girl, showed it. In the end, worn out, Bet retired to bed as soon after supper as she decently could and left them to it. But Bernie of all people ...

At least Jean-Pierre was all right, and seemed delighted with everything. He was a modest, intelligent, unassuming boy, with an attractive sense of humour. Just the sort of friend Bet would have liked for Diz. Liza, on the other hand, when one had recovered from the shock of her beauty, turned out to be both sulky and hard to please, and was plainly used to being the centre of attention. She did not, she told Bet, like dogs or old houses, and complained incessantly of the cold.

It was at breakfast the following morning that she started on about Tib, who with an only too typical lack of tact, had tried to bury his bone under her bed. 'I pull 'im out by 'is tail,' she told the assembled company, 'and 'e growl at me; 'e bites — yes?' 'No,' they chorused in outrage, even Bernie, 'not Tib,' but it was an inauspicious start to the holiday.

Later, Bernie rang from work to say he'd decided to take a few days holiday. 'There's nothing here that can't wait,' he told Bet, 'and I've a load of chores to do at home. Besides,' he added as a careless afterthought, 'I could drive the others around a bit, save them having to hire. They haven't tried to get a car yet?'

'I don't think so, Liza's still in the bath.' Another sore point, this; it was the second time she'd taken all the hot water.

'But why couldn't Bernie have told me himself?' Nell wailed, wide-eyed with suspicion, 'he hasn't any chores, no more than usual, anyway, and the weather's absolutely foul.'

'Bet, if it's still as cold as this, can you tell Christine to turn on the heating on Thursday morning. We'll be arriving around seven on Thursday evening, Pete's got Friday off, so could she also get the grouse out of the deep freeze?'

'Will there be anything else, modom, while you're on the line?'

'Oh Bet, don't be difficult. I've enough on my plate organising this wretched fête. Angela Snately never stops ringing, what her phone bill must be like I dread to think. I thought C. of E. vicars were always supposed to be so poor.' Bet grunted, she was in no mood to listen to moans about the Snatelys, it was Pol's fault for getting involved. Pol, sensing a certain lack of sympathy, pressed on: 'How are the Duponts settling in — are they nice?'

'It depends on what you mean by nice. But this I will say, I would keep Pete on a tight rein if I were you.'

There was a shocked silence at the other end, and Bet smiled in satisfaction. 'You mean Liza Dupont?'

'Yes, dear, I mean Liza Dupont.'
'I see.'

'Mrs Brandon, I am sorry, but I do not eat your cabbage.'
'I'm sorry too, Liza. Perhaps you could have salad instead?'
'That would be most agreeable.'
Liza sat in her chair and lit a Gauloise. Bet went on munching her rissole − let the little b- get her own salad. After a moment or two of rather charged silence, Diz, a bit pink about the gills, sprang to his feet. 'I'll make the salad, Mum, don't you bother.'
'Thanks, darling' − he was a good boy, bless him − 'but I'm afraid you'll have to get a lettuce from the garden, and do make sure you get one from the bed beside the west wall, they've less slugs in them than the others. Liza, dear, would you mind awfully not smoking at meals, it does tend to upset people, especially non-smokers.' Liza, with an aggressive scrape of her chair, also jumped to her feet. 'I will help Dizzy,' she said, and stalked out of the room. JP smiled across at Bet. 'Your cabbage is superb, Mrs Brandon, it is just Liza, she does not ... does not −'
'We can't all like cabbage, JP, if we did there wouldn't be enough to go round, would there?'

'I can't take much more of this, Mum.' Bet and Nell stood at Nell's bedroom window, watching the others pile into Bernie's car. Bernie had just donned Liza's peaked cap and with much hearty laughter − from Bernie and Liza, JP and Diz didn't seem to think it all that funny − Liza was chasing him round the yard trying to get it back. 'Well, darling, I'm afraid there's not a lot we can do about it.' Bet was thoroughly tired of the whole thing, but still doggedly doing her best. 'You should have gone with them. In situations like this you must fight, you know, it's no use sitting back and just letting things take their course.'
'But I feel so ill all the time. It's simply not fair of Bern, I can't think what's got into him.'
'Life isn't fair, darling, you know that. It wasn't fair Dad dying, was it?'

138

'No, of course it wasn't. But Dad never behaved like Bern ... I mean, he just couldn't have.' Bet shrugged. 'We can't know that, can we — after all, he never met Liza.'

Pete was the next to go down; a foregone conclusion this, but if Nell held any hopes that his presence in the house might draw the heat off Bernie, she was doomed to disappointment. Liza was perfectly capable of juggling with any number of suitors, especially when her own feelings were in no way engaged. She privately considered the entire household to be both boring and stupid, and longed to return to Paris. At least the Redford type appeared to be prepared to spend a bit of money, which was more than you could say for the others.

They came together on Friday morning, when Pete found Liza sulking alone on the verandah, lethargically turning the pages of last month's *Vogue*. Diz and JP had gone to lunch with Don Stewart to look at his collection of Neolithic pottery, and being totally uninterested in such things, Liza had elected to stay behind — then discovered, to her considerable annoyance, that Nell, in a rare fit of decisiveness, had taken Bernie out for the day on a long-promised visit to his parents.

'Deserted by your menfolk, Liza? We can't have that now, can we.' Liza shrugged and squinted up at Pete through a haze of Gauloise smoke. 'I do not care. Besides, I 'ave the flu coming on — it is so cold 'ere.'

'I can see you need a bit of cheering up. Why not pop into Stourwick with me and have a bite of lunch? I have to go there anyway, to do a bit of shopping for my wife.' Liza, after a quick glance at the gleaming Aston Martin crouched outside the front door, stubbed out her cigarette and stretched. 'Why not?' she said, putting out a heavily ringed brown claw. Pete, his heart beating a little too fast for comfort, took it and pulled her to her feet. 'That,' he said, in his excitement reverting to the vernacular of his youth, 'would be absolutely smashing.'

Bet, delighted to get rid of Liza and enjoying a solitary glass of beer and a cheese sandwich, was rudely interrupted by her sister. 'Pete's just rung to say he's giving that wretched girl lunch at the White Hart — can you beat it? I didn't even know she'd gone to Stourwick with him.' Bet took a bite of sandwich. 'Well, I did tell you, didn't I – that girl's dynamite.'

'But how dare he. Pete never does things like that. There I am getting our lunch after a gruelling two hours with the tea committee, when he rings as cool as you please to say he and Liza have been delayed, so he's giving her a quick lunch at the White Hart. Then before I can say anything, he's rung off.'

Bet, unable to stop herself, snorted. She hadn't meant to sound derisive, but as usual Pol took it the wrong way. 'I might have known I'd get no sympathy from you! But just you wait till that harpy claps eyes on that boyfriend of yours. And while I'm here, Bet, may I ask you once again to make sure Tib keeps out of our part of the house; I found dog's hairs all over the sofa this morning ...'

After she'd gone, feeling defiant Bet took another swig of beer and switched on the radio. But somehow she couldn't concentrate; Pol's taunt had gone home. But she needn't worry, surely. Simon wasn't down, was he, and Liza returned to France on Wednesday. Oh God, Simon ... Suddenly she didn't feel hungry any more; Tib could have her sandwich.

'Rather a fancy piece, the boy's sister?' Don Stewart, sleeves rolled up, was helping Bet clear away Saturday lunch, while the rest of the party hunted for the croquet set. The weather was fine at last, and croquet seemed as good a way as any of keeping the young amused.

'That's one way of putting it, I suppose.' At least there was one male immune to the bloody girl's charms. 'In the short time she's been here she's already managed to stir up an amazing amount of trouble. Though thank God, I have a feeling Diz is beginning to see the light. Liza doesn't like dogs, and he caught her throwing stones at Tib.'

'Thank God for dogs ... Shall I take the tray?'

'Thanks.' Bet, comforted, followed him on to the verandah where Pol and Pete were already drinking their coffee.

For a few short minutes all was peace; four middle-aged people sat chatting companionably in the sun, waiting to watch their young at play. But all too soon Diz and JP appeared, bustling with enthusiasm, hurrying across the lawn to place the croquet hoops; lagging behind, not helping, were

140

Bernie, Liza − in a brilliant red shirt and the briefest of brief shorts − and Nell, looking miserable. Nell went and plonked herself down beside her mother.

'Not playing then, darling?'

'No, I don't feel too good, actually. Anyway, only four can play croquet, and I can't see Bern dropping out, can you?'

'Perhaps not, but I'm sure Diz wouldn't mind letting you take his place −'

'Oh, can it, Mum. I don't want to play anyway, so please don't go on.' Pete winked at Bet, who frowned and shook her head. He was just as bad as Bernie, only more crafty.

The game began at last; Pete and Don lay back in their chairs and prepared for a post-prandial nap, Nell and Pol immersed themselves in the Sunday supplements and Bet, unable to settle and finding herself too hot, decided she needed a hat. Rounding the corner of the house on her way to get one, she was just in time to see Simon's car turn in at the gate and pull up at the front door. Stopped in her tracks, with a mixture of despair and stomach-churning excitement she watched him emerge from the car, slam the door behind him, and catching sight of her standing under the cedar tree, smile and walk towards her. 'Hullo, Titania. Hope I'm not interrupting anything; by the number of cars in the back yard I thought there might be another party going on.'

'Only Don Stewart to lunch. When did you get down?'

'Late last night. I'm taking a few days off work, I've had just about as much of that place as I can stand.'

'I expect they'll manage to soldier on without you. They must be used to it by now, you hardly ever seem to be there.' Now why did she have to go and say that; why start off on the wrong foot − why? Simon stopped smiling.

'If you say so. But at least I do occasionally work for my living, which is more than one can say for some.'

'Meaning I sit about on my arse all day doing nothing, I suppose?'

'Meaning damn all! And if you're going to be boring, darling, I'm off. I only looked for a moment anyway, just to see how you were coping with the French.'

It was at this inauspicious moment that Pete just happened to step out from behind a rose bush. 'Hullo, there, Morris, long time no see.' Had he been listening? Knowing Pete, yes. 'Come and join us on the verandah and soak up a bit of sun,' Pete put an avuncular arm on Simon's shoulder. 'Marvellous day, isn't it. How's your French, by the way, or more to the point, how's your croquet? The kids need someone to make up the numbers.'

'I can just about get by with my French.' Far from looking annoyed at the interruption, Simon seemed delighted. 'I once did a spell as a croupier at the casino in Monte Carlo. Not so sure about my croquet – haven't played in years ...' And Bet, blightingly aware that whatever was happening was entirely her own fault, left them to it and went in search of her hat.

Ten minutes later, after hunting all over the house for the hat, a rather becoming broad-brimmed red straw purchased years ago from Oxfam, and found at last rather squashed under a pile of mackintoshes in the downstairs loo. Bet returned to the verandah. Though she said so herself, she looked really rather pretty in the hat; she felt chastened in spirit, and ready to apologise for previous churlishness.

She was too late.

The thing she had dreaded ever since the Duponts' arrival in Suffolk was well on its way to happening. Liza, after an unsatisfactory game partnered by Bernie – she hated losing – had returned sulkily to the grown-ups in search of further prey and was about to be introduced to Simon. Pol, perfidious Pol, was performing the necessary introductions. 'Simon, this is Liza Dupont, her English is slightly short of perfect, so I'm sure she'll be delighted to meet someone who speaks really decent French. The rest of us are rather lacking in that department I'm afraid.' It was of course a meeting of Titans – Titans in the game of love, that is, not in much else. And when it was over, Bet, watching impotent and miserable from the sidelines, felt the only thing left for her to do was hurl herself and her stupid hat into the nearest litter bin.

'Will you be my partner, Mister Morris? Bernie, 'e is no good at this croquet.' Liza, twisting the silver bangle on her arm, had her head back, and was squinting up at Simon through the longest, most perfectly curling eyelashes this side of the Ural Mountains. Simon, acknowledging her signals, and sending out so many of his own that he resembled nothing so much as an illuminated traffic beacon on a foggy night, was saying Yes, he would be delighted to have a go, but not to count on him as he hadn't played croquet in years and was probably no better than Bernie. Than they lapsed into fast, idiomatic French which no one else could follow, but which was obviously frightfully funny as he and Liza both fell about laughing.

It was at this point that Simon saw Bet and had the effrontery to wink. 'I like the hat, Titania, you should wear one more often. I hope you're going to watch the match and see me give these kids a thrashing?' But Bet was not to be drawn, such patronising tactics not for her. 'It's a pleasure I'm afraid I shall have to forego,' she said, trying not to look at Liza's hand on his arm, 'Don and I are about to get tea.' Don looking surprised, leapt to his feet, and Simon for one brief, blissful instant looked rather annoyed.

The bastard, the selfish, miserable, callous bastard, Don thought to himself as he hurried after Bet. But to be absolutely honest, he did find it all rather exciting, and despite the slightly dubious morality of the thought, he had to admit that one man's defection could quite possibly be turned into another man's opportunity.

'You see,' Pol said, 'I knew this would happen.' The Redfords and Nell were left alone amidst the empty coffee cups, listening to the renewed laughter from the croquet pitch.

'In that case, you must be pleased you've been proved right.'

'For heaven's sake, Pete, I don't like watching my sister being humiliated, even if you do.'

'Come off it, ducky, the chap's only gone to play a game of croquet.'

'You come off it, Uncle Pete.' This from Nell, not knowing whether to be pleased or sorry. 'It's a bit more than that; I mean, it was absolutely blatant.'

'I don't know what you're worrying about, then, at least it means old Bern is off the hook — '

'Bernie's never been on the hook! He was just practising his French, he has this business trip to Brussels next year and — '

'Of course Bernie has to practise his French, dear, it's only common sense when he gets such a marvellous chance.' Pol gently patted her scowling niece's arm. 'And you're a sweet, good, plucky girl and he doesn't deserve you.' Pete snorted. 'I'm warning you, Pete,' Pol rounded on her trouble-making spouse, 'if you say one more word I shan't be responsible for the consequences.' Pete, feeling rebellious, snorted again, and then with a shrug immersed himself in the Sunday newspaper.

After that there was silence.

'Sorry about the phone call the other afternoon, Titania,' Simon said as, game over — Simon and Liza triumphant winners — they all gathered round for tea. 'I understand I was a little drunk. I got dragged off to this party and — '

'Spare me the details,' Bet said, 'and as you're here, perhaps you wouldn't mind handing round the sandwiches.'

Compulsive sandwich-making had always been one of the things Bet did when in a state of tension, it seemed to have a therapeutic effect on her. However, today's stint turned out to be the exception that proved the rule. Despite having produced enough sandwiches to furnish a school outing, she felt just as bad as ever.

Pol, not to be outdone, had produced a lemon sponge. 'Made by a little woman in Peabody Buildings,' she told the assembled company, 'a Mrs Jobling. She used to be cook to Lady Lauderdale — *the* Lady Lauderdale — and although she's over eighty now, she still likes to keep her hand in. She's incredibly cheap, you just supply the ingredients.' But nobody took Pol up, and her remarks on Lady Lauderdale's ex-cook were greeted in damp silence. Despite the delicious food, the tea party just wasn't working. Liza Dupont looked about her with satisfaction; she thrived on situations such as this, all her life it had been so.

'Back to work on Monday, more's the pity.' Everyone looked at Bernie in surprise, he was not normally given to plunging alone into a conversational vacuum; things really must be desperate. 'Yes,' Nell contributed her mite, 'I expect it'll be quite a rest for you after all you've done. Incidentally, those chores you said were waiting for you to do at home — what exactly were they?'

'Anyone for a drink?' Pete was obviously beginning to wilt.

144

Simon looked up from his contemplation of the little golden hairs on Liza's legs. 'I wouldn't say no.'

'Nonsense.' Pol put her foot down, 'it's much too early. Would anyone like another cup of tea?' No one wanted another cup of tea and Nell rose from her chair rather quickly. 'I think I'm going to be sick.'

'What's that, pet?' Bernie hovered, looking pained. 'For goodness sake go after her, can't you see she needs you?' Bernie looked at Pol, surprised. 'All right, but she usually likes to be alone when she's being sick.'

At this point Don Stewart decided he'd had enough, at least for the time being. He was begining to feel like a character in a Chekhov play, his role, he reflected gloomily, that of the drunken doctor. 'Look, I must be going, I've stayed far too long as it is, I've the proofs of my book to go through and a man's coming to look at the chimney at six.' Simon roused himself. 'It's time I went too.'

'Oh, do not go yet, Mister Morris, let us play another game. It is early.'

'No, really, I must get back.' He smiled at Bet. If this was his idea of making amends, he had another think coming; she turned away to collect up the cups. 'I tell you what,' Simon said, taking no notice, 'why doesn't anyone who can, come over to tea at the Manor tomorrow? Cyn will be out, but Alfonso and I between us could probably rustle up the odd stale bun. I could look out the croquet gear and perhaps we could have a return match.'

'Oh, Mister Morris . . . to 'ave tea in an old English Manor . . . that would be marvellous.'

'I thought you said you didn't like old houses, Liza?'

'This is different, Mrs Brandon, this is Mister Morris's manor 'House.'

'There is a spider in my bedroom, Mrs Brandon.'

'Oh dear.'

'I do not like spiders, Mrs Brandon, please arrange for it to go away.'

'My dear Liza, I'm not particularly fond of spiders myself, but in the country you simply have to learn to get used to them.' JP and Diz had gone to the pub, the Sparsworths, worn out from quarrelling, were having an early night, and Liza had just emerged from one of her interminable baths.

'Spiders I cannot get used to.'

'In that case I really don't know what to suggest. Perhaps you'd better wait downstairs until Diz and your brother get back, they shouldn't be long, but please don't wake the others, Nell needs all the sleep she can get.' Liza, looking as if she would like to have said a whole lot more but didn't quite dare to, shrugged, and stalked off downstairs, the heels of her little gold slippers clacking aggressively on the bare boards. She was wearing orange towelling pyjamas, and her hair, wet from the bath, was tied in a topknot on her head; she looked totally and utterly stunning.

Shortly afterwards, Bet was sitting by her open bedroom window looking out on the moonswept grass and sniffing the scent of honeysuckle, when she heard Pol's voice – Pete must have been called to the rescue and she wasn't letting him out of her sight. 'Really, one would have thought there might be somebody in this house not afraid of spiders. Now I come to think of it, what about Bet, she loves them, it's bats she doesn't like ...'

Bet smiled into the darkness.

Chapter Thirteen

In the end no one played croquet. When the somewhat depleted rectory party arrived at the Manor the following afternoon – Nell had put her foot down, and the Sparsworths had stayed behind – they were informed by Simon, who for some reason looked rather jaded, that the grass was too long; Old Tom, whose job it was to cut it, was away on his annual summer holidays. The revolutionary idea that Simon himself might perhaps have stepped into the breach and done the mowing, had plainly never occurred to him, and even Pol lacked the gall to suggest it. 'Anyway,' he told them as they ranged themselves round the rather charming summerhouse in which the tea had been laid out, 'there seems to be only one croquet mallett, and most of the hoops have disappeared. How about a tour of inspection instead?'

Tea, to everyone's surprise, turned out to be pretty impressive; wafer-thin bread and butter, seed cake and sandwiches, two different jams, and the tea itself served in a silver teapot, scented and delicious. 'Not quite the stale buns you promised us, Morris?'

'Well, you see, Alfonso's currently anti Cyn; when he's anti Cyn, he's pro me; that's how he operates. Now, if Cyn were to have had a tea party today, it would have been stale buns and the tin teapot; probably used tea-bags to boot. He once served that up to Bonzo Harrington, and the poor old devil nearly had a seizure.' Pol sniffed. No menial of hers would be allowed to exercise temperament in such a way. The West-overs, however, seemed to think it all frightfully funny. Never mind, she had to admit that the man certainly knew his business when in the right mood.

After tea the Duponts and Diz accepted Simon's offer of a tour, but the others opted out, Pol because she felt it smacked of the bourgeois to tramp round other people's property, even though one's guide was a member of the family; Pete because he couldn't be bothered, and the sight of Liza's bottom under her tight pink jeans bobbing up and down in front of him might prove too great a strain on a hot afternoon. And Bet because she was fed up.

'Come on, Titania, don't be a spoilsport, you'll enjoy it.' Simon held out his hand, and Bet was about to change her mind when Liza butted in and spoiled it. 'Titania, Simon, why do you call Dizzy's mother this?' she said, putting an arm round his waist and smiling mockingly at Bet. 'It would take too long to explain.' Simon was still looking at Bet, but as she refused to look at him, the moment passed. 'Mrs Brandon is tired, Simon, can you not see? She does not want to come.'

'Well, and do they have anything like this in France, then?'

The question was, of course, purely rhetorical; he was quite sure they didn't. Simon, torn between attraction and distraction, was alone with Liza in the old melon and cucumber house, a long, low, brick building, warm and dim as the inside of a cow, so choked with memories of past entanglements — indeed 'I took her (or him) to the cu' house' in the days of their youth had been his and Cyn's secret code for illicit sex — it was suffocating. 'When I was a boy,' he went on as Liza remained silent, 'the melon and cucumber plants climbed right up to the roof like a vine. Hundreds of cucumbers there were, all hanging down like great big phalluses. When we were small, Cyn and I played jungles in here. Later on . . . well . . . other things.'

Liza, bored by all these reminiscences, picked up a feather used by Old Tom for the purposes of pollination, and tickled Simon's ear with it. 'Why do you not make love to me, Simon?' Simon took the feather away and removed her questing hand, the sense of déjà vu now so powerful he wanted to scream. 'Because I have things on my mind; anyway not now and certainly not in here. Anyone might pop in at any minute, and what about the boys?'

Liza's face took on an ill-tempered expression and she began to tear the leaves off a melon plant. 'It is Dizzy's mother you are afraid of, not the boys. I see the way she looks at you — me, I know these things.' Simon closed his eyes. God, how he hated women sometimes! 'Don't talk rubbish, and for Christ's sake leave the melons alone. Old Tom will kill us both if anything happens to them, they're all he has left.'

'You are master here, Simon, not this Old Tom.' Liza put her arms round his neck and wiggled her hips against his. 'In France we do not treat our servants in this way.'

'I'm not master here, my cousin is, and anyway Old Tom's not a servant. Now, for heaven's sake stop being tiresome and come and help me find the boys.' Liza searched crossly in her shoulder bag and produced a crumpled packet of Gauloises: 'It is you who are tiresome! Go then, if you wish, but I shall remain here and smoke my cigarette.'

'All right then, I will! But aren't you being rather childish?' Feeling slightly silly — odd how often this seemed to happen these days — and hoping that at the last minute she would change her mind, Simon made for the door. She didn't, but sitting herself down on an upturned bucket, watched him derisively through a cloud of smoke. 'Go then, and find your Mrs Brandon, Simon, it is sure she will be waiting for you!' And Simon, who could cheerfully have garrotted her, shrugged his shoulders and went.

Liza, listening to his receding footsteps, puffed at her cigarette and waited confidently for his return. Men never walked away from her — never. Especially men who looked at her in the way Simon did. He was playing a deep game, that one! Never mind, it was more fun this way . . .

Five minutes later, with still no sign of Simon, she was not so sure. She got up from the bucket, stretched, threw her cigarette stub on the floor and decided to pay him out — and incidentally boring Old Tom as well — by plucking a few choice melon flowers to put in her hair. It was just as she'd finished doing this and was admiring her reflection in a handy pane of glass, that once again there were footsteps on the stone path outside the shed. So . . . he had given in, he could not keep away from her! How delicious to have power such as

149

this. She waited in triumph for the door of the shed to open.

But when it did open, it was not Simon who stood there framed in the doorway, but a young man Liza had never seen before. A young man incomprehensibly carrying a pair of scissors, and of such surpassing good looks that he quite took her breath away. It was Alfonso, come to cut a melon for that night's supper — but she did not know that until later.

For a long moment they looked at one another, the gorgeous Spaniard twirling his scissors, and the equally gorgeous French girl fingering the yellow melon flowers in her hair. It was Alfonso who spoke first, his voice, as Liza had known it would be, low, thrilling and sexy, his English no better than her own.

'The senorita, she is lost? I show her ...?'

Liza shook her head, and proffered her packet of Gauloises. 'No, I am not lost,' she said in tolerably fluent Spanish, grateful for once to Maman for those six months spent in Madrid with boring Dr Gonzales and his even more boring family; at the time she'd vowed vengance on Maman for such an act of treachery to her only daughter, however, for once Maman had been proved right. 'But do, please, show me ...'

'Dizzy, we should return, perhaps?'

'I suppose so, but honestly, J.P., what a place! This stuff must have been here since before the First World War.' Diz and JP were in the old harness room; Diz, with cobwebs in his hair, was peering into a cupboard. 'Christ, here's a bottle of the Westover horse stuff! That's what they made their money in, you know.' He emerged from the cupboard, triumphantly clutching a large bottle filled with what looked like green slime. However, a yellowing label still adhering to the side proclaimed its contents to be Hopton's Magic Equine Elixir. And, just to make sure no one was in any doubt as to its magical powers, there were two pictures, one showing a horse lying down in the last stages of terminal illness, the other the same horse, presumably having been dosed, jumping exuberantly over a five-barred gate.

'I say, I wonder if Simon knows about this cupboard, it doesn't look as if anyone's opened it in years. Let's go and

150

find him, he and Liza must be around somewhere.'

Cautiously JP pulled the cork from the bottle and sniffed, but Hopton's Magic Elixir had somehow lost its potency; it simply smelt of nothing. 'Let us return to your mother and Mr and Mrs Redford,' he said, carefully replacing the cork, 'they will be wondering where we are.' He had no desire to hunt for Liza. He knew his sister, he'd come upon her once before in a compromising situation and she didn't like it.

'No need to go back yet, JP, after all Simon did take us on a tour of the place and there's masses more to see ...' Arguing amicably, they emerged into the sunlit stable yard. Of Liza and Simon there was no sign; only Alfonso in mufti, a cigar between his teeth, watching them from his flat above the kitchens, and an elderly labrador lying asleep in the shelter of the barn door.

Bet, alone in the summerhouse with the remains of the tea, was feeling sorry for herself. She'd refused to go with Pol and Pete, who had wandered off round the garden on their own tour of inspection, and there was no sign of the rest of the party. For a while she'd heard distant shouts and laughter, but these had died away long since, and now there was only silence. She felt like a naughty child put in the corner, the only difference being – idiot that she was – that she'd put herself there. Mothers of grown-up children weren't supposed to behave like this; childish sulks were simply not on the agenda. She watched miserably as a fly settled on the remains of the seed cake, and tried unsuccessfully not to think what Simon at this very moment was doing to Liza – or what Liza was doing to Simon; who did it to whom was immaterial. Oh God!

'Good heavens, it's Mrs Brandon – I thought I saw somebody.' It was Cyn, radiating health and smelling slightly of cow dung. Bet leapt to her feet. 'Miss Westover.'

'Call me Cyn, my dear, everyone does.'

'Er, Cyn, Simon asked us to tea, I don't know if he told you? We were supposed to be playing croquet, but there didn't seem to be any malletts and he said the grass was too long, so he's taken the others on a tour of inspection instead. I do hope that's all right?' Cyn gave one of her raucous laughs. 'Of course it's all right, although there's precious little to see these days, the whole place seems to be going to rack and ruin. The thing is, I'm up to my ears in horses all the time, and Si's never here.' Bet was aware of being scrutinised, and that Cyn's brown eyes were surprisingly like Simon's; odd she hadn't noticed it before. 'Left you behind, did they, the meanies, or didn't you fancy a tour of inspection?'

'Well, I felt a bit tired actually – having a houseful of people can be rather exhausting.'

'Wouldn't know, thank God, I leave all that sort of thing to Alfonso, bless him. By the way, what sort of tea did he produce?' Bet pointed silently to the sumptuous remains laid out on the summerhouse table. Cyn whistled. 'So that's the way the wind blows. We can only hope he's still on form when the Lord Lieutenant comes next week – for all our sakes.' She gave Bet another sharp look. 'Now then, my dear, you look as though you could do with a drink and I'm damned sure I could, I've had the most ghastly afternoon.'

'Should I clear up a bit?' Bet gestured timidly towards the tea things, now buzzing happily with flies. 'Heavens no, that's Alfonso's pigeon. If he was stupid enough to bring all this stuff out here, he can jolly well take it back. Come on.'

Pleased for any diversion, Bet followed her hostess back across the little lawn, where in the middle Eros still danced away on his pedestal. Only today he seemed to be laughing. Had he been there too that summer in the far away thirties, when Simon's parents made love? He looked as though he'd witnessed a good many strange goings on in his time; the prolonged effect of wind, weather and countless bird droppings had combined to give his face a slightly raffish, slightly lascivious air which Bet was sure the sculptor hadn't intended.

As she followed Cyn through the French window into the morning room, she tried not to look at the broken-down sofa on the verandah on which Simon had made love to her; that too seemed to be mocking her, and she didn't think she could bear it.

Cyn waved an arm. 'Sit down – that's if you can find a space, I'm afraid the place is a bit of a shambles.' Bet, obeying, became aware of something hard and sharp sticking into her behind that on investigation turned out to be a minute tin racehorse, a brightly-coloured jockey crouching on its back. She held the thing up. 'I seem to have sat on something.'

'Hurray – another one's turned up! It's that wretched Simon, he lost his temper the other night playing Totopoly and threw the whole lot at me – he simply loathes losing, you see. It's a bloody nuisance, the dice have completely disappeared and we've still only managed to find half the horses. I think Alfonso must have hoovered the rest up. Drink all right?' Bet gulped her gin and tonic, and the strength of the gin made her eyes water. 'Yes, thank you,' she said, stroking the marmalade dog's ears. Unlike most other people, he seemed to like her, and had placed a tentative paw on her knee. 'Kick him off if he's a bore. Oxford's one of those dogs who find it impossible to believe there are people around who actually don't think he's the best thing since sliced bread.'

'Please don't worry – I love dogs. They always seem so simple and straightforward . . . compared with people.'

'Don't let you down, yes, I know what you mean.' Cyn took a swig at her drink, and plonking herself down in a green armchair that had seen better days, smiled across at Bet. Bet smiled back, then looked at the floor; she felt like a fourth-former waiting to have a pijaw with the head prefect.

There followed a long, long silence, broken only by the thump of Oxford's tail on the carpet and the scrabble of his paws on Bet's best blue linen skirt. Then, just as the silence seemed to be about to stretch into infinity, Cyn, having topped up her tonic with another gin, said: 'Look, my dear, I know it's none of my damned business, but don't let Si get you down. He's a most fearful tease, you know, always has been.' Well, that was one way of putting it. 'I'm not defending him, but he did have rather a rough time as a child – I don't know if he's told you about it, but I sometimes think it affected him a bit. I'm no shrink – heaven forbid – never see anything further than the end of my nose most of the time, but Si's a good sort underneath, and I think it did.'

Could she take all this? It was hard enough to cope anyway. Bet said, 'Actually, he has told me a little. He –'

'Of course he never knew his father, and he and my Aunt Nance didn't get on. He simply refused point-blank to live

153

with her, you know, when he was a kid; just kept on buggering back here. Nearly drove poor old Pa round the bend. Pa gave in in the end, hadn't much choice. Besides, as he said, you couldn't blame anyone not wanting to live with Aunt Nance, let alone Uncle Toby. Anyway, what all this spiel's in aid of is ... Si is just, well, Si, and it's too late to change him.'

Another silence, while Bet took a gulp of her drink and felt the gin fizzing through her veins and giving her false courage. As she placed her glass carefully down on the little table beside her chair – the table was shaped like an elephant, with a brass tray on its back – out of the corner of her eye she saw the figures of her son, JP and Simon walking across the lawn towards the house. There was no sign of Liza; presumably Simon, in a grotesque effort to keep up appearances, had told the girl to make her own way back. 'I've never wanted to change anybody in my life,' she said, looking Cyn straight in the eye and knowing even as she said it that it was an empty boast. She was just as much of a fraud as everyone else; she *had* wanted to change someone. She had, she had, she had ...

At that moment the morning room door opened to reveal Liza, her skin the colour of ripe apples, her horrible, snaky hair dripping water on to the carpet. 'I took a shower, it was so 'ot in the stable ... Alphonse, 'e show me. Where are Simon and the boys?'

And then, to crown it all, Pete entered left, waving a broken-stringed tennis racket of antediluvian design, and wearing an even more antediluvian cricket cap on his head. 'Anyone for tennis?'

But by now Bet had had enough. She hated the lot of them, including Pete. She closed her eyes, only to find that the room seemed to be spinning round inside her head; somewhere in the distance was the buzzing of a thousand bees. 'I think I'm going to faint,' she said in a loud, clear voice, and passed flat out on the carpet.

'Si?'

'Umm.'

'What are you going to do about the Brandon woman?'

'Check. You shouldn't talk so much while you're playing,

154

it spoils the concentration, that's why you always lose.'

'I don't always lose, and you haven't answered my question.' Cyn, with little hope of saving him, moved her king out of harm's way and waited.

'Checkmate, and I'm not going to do anything about the Brandon woman, as you call her,' Simon said, not looking at Cyn and getting up to pour himself another drink.

'But you do care for her, don't you. Come on, admit it.'

'Of course I care for her; I always care for them, don't I?'

. 'You mean you don't care for her any longer?'

'Look, what the hell's got into you tonight? It's not like you to play the agony aunt.'

'Nothing's got into me. It's just, well ... That French girl this afternoon ... Hitting a bit below the belt, isn't it?'

'Rather an unfortunate turn of phrase —'

'Don't be a bore, Si, you know exactly what I mean.'

'Am I being treated to a lecture on morals, darling — a bit late in the day, isn't it?'

'Of course you're not being treated to a lecture on morals, you ass. It's only that I was just beginning to think it might be on the cards you'd really fallen for the Brandon woman, that's all. Then you suddenly start argy-bargying about with the French bit. OK, the French bit's a corker, even I can see that, but you must have met dozens like her, and —'

'There's no need to go all round the houses. What exactly are you driving at?' Si was beginning to get ratty, Cyn could see the warning signs, but somehow tonight she didn't care. He hated talking about his love life, especially to her. The trouble was that in their dealings with each other, she and Si were still stuck in the nursery, circa 1947. She wasn't knocking their relationship, wouldn't dream of it, it was the most important thing in her life. But — and it came to her with a flash of insight almost unprecedented — it did somehow seem to have got stuck; and perhaps, she wasn't entirely sure, but perhaps this wasn't all that good for either of them.

'Come on then, you can't start something and not go through with it ...' Si's left foot had begun to tap, and he was making little triangles with some matches he'd tipped out of the big matchbox on the sofa table. Any minute now he'd go into one of his tantrums − a bad one by the look of it, like that time he'd smashed up her dollshouse furniture with a hammer. But it was no good, she had to press on. 'What I suppose I'm trying to say is, that I thought you might be going to do a "Caroline" over again, and if you were − and I'm not blaming you if you did, you can't help your black monkey, as Nanny always said − but if you were ... well, it would be rather bad luck on Mrs Brandon.'

There followed a long silence in which Oxford, poised for a quick getaway, looked ingratiatingly from one to the other. In the event, all that happened was that Simon, having carefully re-packed the matches in their box, stood up rather suddenly, and looking hard at the portrait of Mrs Saltpeter Westover on the opposite wall, and in a voice cold enough to freeze a brass monkey at forty paces, said: 'If all you can do is talk bloody nonsense, I'm off to bed,' and banged out of the room, slamming the door as hard as he could behind him.

'Damn and blast!' If Cyn had been the sort of girl who cried, she would have cried now. As it was she simply sat on the sofa with Oxford cuddled up beside her, drank her drink and wished with all her might that she were dead.

Driving back to London on a badly congested A12 the following morning, Simon felt not much better. And the fact that he'd been ordered to London forthwith by his director − who, when Simon informed him over the phone that morning that he was taking a few days well-earned rest, had said that if he wasn't in the office by mid-day he needn't bother coming back − was by no means the sole reason for his gloom.

Most of it was due to Bet.

How could one feel guilty and furious at the same time, and on top of that, dislike oneself so intensely? Guilty − and guilt had never been one of his things − for having started the affair with Bet in the first place; and furious because although he should never have started it, once he *had* embarked on it, by his own admittedly abysmal standards he'd behaved rather well, and therefore didn't see why he *should* feel guilty. The disliking himself a bit was nothing new; he'd never been much of an admirer of Simon Morris, and not infrequently found himself wondering what on earth it was other people seemed to see in him.

156

He also felt rather sad.

Cyn, as usual, was right. She'd said it would end in tears. And it wasn't because of the French piece, either, but because Bet just wasn't the sort of woman you could have a fling with. He'd known that, really, and so had she, but brave, funny girl that she was, she'd had a go and got badly mauled in the process. Christ, what a shit he was! But shit or not, there was a part of him that loved Bet, and he hadn't loved a woman, really loved a woman, since Caroline.

Caroline . . . Old Cyn had been right about her too, damn her. Funnily enough, he'd seen a photograph of Caroline only the other day in a copy of *Country Life* at the dentist's. It had given him quite a turn; it had also made him feel old. The photo showed her looking distinctly matronly − he even detected the hint of a double chin − seated in an extremely posh drawing-room with a pair of supercilious labradors and a rather wet-looking teenage daughter. She had apparently just written a book on the role of the younger son in English nineteenth-century fiction − hardly a subject to set the Thames on fire, one would have thought, but at least she'd completed it, which was more than you could say of his own puny literary efforts. She had also, so the blurb informed anyone interested, recently been made chairwoman of her local Marriage Guidance Council, and regularly opened her garden to the public in aid of War on Want.

In fact − and the thought came to him just as he was girding up the loins of his elderly Volkswagen in order to overtake the leaky-looking juggernaut in front of him, which had been monopolising the middle lane for the past inter- minable five minutes − these were exactly the type of busybodying activities that Bet, given half the chance, would be only too happy to get up to herself. And what that proved, he didn't exactly know, except perhaps that the only two women in the last twenty years for whom he'd cared a tuppeny damn were tarred with the same brush. In other words, they were both self-opinionated, bossy do-gooders who should never have had anything to do with someone like him in the first place.

This conclusion to his musings, interesting though it was, somehow failed to make Simon feel any better − although the juggernaut driver's two-fingered salute as the Volkswagen roared past him, did — and he decided to occupy the remainder of the journey thinking about something else. Like whether to jack in Smike McGregor now, before they jacked him in, or go for broke and ask for a rise. The latter course, though drastic, had been known to work. People were so surprised that they gave in before they had time to think what they were doing. And he did need a new car, there was no question but that his present heap was on its last legs, despite Sid Kettle's ministrations . . . On balance, though, he thought perhaps he'd jack it in . . .

Thus Simon, bogged down with his worries and deep in thought, ground on towards London.

Chapter Fourteen

For Bet, things were even worse. Already punch-drunk by the events of the previous day's tea party at the Manor, she'd barely had time to sit up and take notice before she was knocked for six again by two further disasters.

The first — bad, but not as bad as the second — was the arrival on Monday morning of a reply-paid telegram from the Dupont parents in Antibes. The gist of which was, Would chère Madame Brandon mind hanging on to Liza for another six days? Business affairs of an unexpected nature having delayed Monsieur Dupont in the south, the Paris apartment would remain shut up until next week. Well, what could one say? One could scarcely refuse — not in a telegram, anyway — on the grounds that Liza was in all probability being screwed by chère Madame Brandon's lover and Madame Brandon didn't like it. One really had no choice but to say yes with as good a grace as one could muster under the circumstances, and hope without much conviction that the wretched girl would make no more trouble than she'd succeeded in doing already.

There was one consolation. Apart from Bernie — and even he was showing signs of strain; he'd developed a nervous tic in one eye, and appeared to have lost at least a stone in weight — the rest of the household were as depressed by the news of Liza's prolonged stay in their midst as Bet herself. Pol said that if it wasn't for the fête, she'd have cut short Pete's holiday. Nell made a noise like a peacock in pain and said, 'Mum, you must be mad.' JP went pale, and Diz said, 'Oh God, Mum, must she?' as though the whole thing were Bet's fault.

159

Liza, when finally tracked down in the vegetable garden where she was doing a spot of topless sunbathing, said it was OK by her, and went on massaging suntan oil into her already perfectly bronzed legs. Bet, bursting with frustration and spoiling for a row, said Well, that was all right then, but she would just like to say this. If Liza was to stay on she, Bet, would be grateful if Liza (a) made her bed each morning, (b) gave an occasional hand with the washing-up, and (c) refrained from filling her bath to the brim each night and thus depriving the rest of the household of hot water.

Liza, shrugging gracefully, said there would be no necessity for her to assist in the washing-up as from now on she would be eating out. A friend from Paris had just happened to turn up and was staying in Stourwick; it would be convenient for all, would it not, if she spent her time at his place? (A friend from Paris – was this Simon's idea of a joke?) As to her bed, Liza went on to say, sitting up and starting on her shoulders despite the pointlessness of such an exercise, she would be prepared to make it each morning, if chère Madame Brandon, for her part, agreed to keep her dog shut up, or at least under control. Only yesterday she had caught the creature in her bedroom, pulling things from her rucksack.

Bet, longing to shove Liza's bottle of suntan lotion down her throat, somehow, heaven knew how, kept her temper and her dignity. She had no intention whatever, she said kindly but firmly, of keeping Tib shut up, Liza must simply try to remember to keep her bedroom door closed. And if she were intending to be out for most of her meals, perhaps she would be good enough to inform Bet well in advance when she was eating in, thus making the task of housekeeping so much easier, as she was sure Liza must agree. It would be sad indeed, she went on, warming to her subject, would it not, if she, Bet, were compelled to tell chère Madame Dupont that her darling daughter was being rather less than co-operative.

Liza responded by sighing heavily, wriggling over on to her stomach – exposing her bottom to anyone who just might be watching, and Bet was pretty sure she saw an upstairs curtain twitch – and sticking her transistor radio earphones into her ears, thus bringing the audience to an end, and causing Bet, baffled but unbeaten, to retire to the kitchen. There was one crumb of comfort, though, she told herself, to calm her exacerbated nerves; if Liza disliked her as much as she appeared to do − Bet disliked Liza, of course, but then who wouldn't − it must be in part because she was jealous of her, and if that were so, well, at least it was something, wasn't it? That was the first disaster.

The second occurred a little over twenty-four hours later. This time was spent by Bet in trying to be resigned about Simon, who naturally hadn't got in touch; in coping as best she could with her guests, her despair, and the frequent calls on her time made by her wretched sister who needed her help in preparing for the fête; and in listening to her tiresome daughter who, with Liza off her back and morning sickness a thing of the past, did nothing but witter on about baby clothes, her own housewifely duties, and any other thing that happened to crop up. The only bright spot in all this was that, true to her word, and apart from gulping down a cup of black coffee when she surfaced on Tuesday morning, Liza was mercifully absent.

On the Tuesday evening Bet ate *en famille* with the Redfords − yet another olive branch from Pol; the boys were out enjoying themselves, Nell and Bernie were having coffee with friends, and Liza was God knew where. Returning from supper, Bet was met by Diz. 'Where's Tib, Mum? He wasn't here when JP and I got back, we thought he must be with you.' But he wasn't with Bet, she never took Tib to the Redfords, Pol was always such a bore about him.

It was only hours later, when they abandoned the fruitless search until morning and went sadly upstairs to bed, that they discovered Liza had been in her room all the time. Of course, they asked her in the morning if Tib had been there when she returned to the Rectory last night. No, she did not think so; she had not felt too good, her friend had had to get back so she'd come home early and gone to bed. She had thought the dog must be with Madame Brandon next door. Now if they would excuse her, she must hurry to catch her bus.

All that day they hunted for Tib. They rang the police, they rang the RSPCA, they even rang old Monty Cornwall. Helpers were roped in − Don Stewart, Ron Stokes, Mr Bone − and up in the seclusion of her bedroom Bet looked at

Tib's empty basket and cried as she had not done since, as a child, her puppy, Masterson, was knocked over and killed in the road outside their house.

Then, in the evening, rummaging through the rubbish sack, she found an empty box of chocolates that bore unmistakable signs of having been chewed by a dog. The box belonged to Liza, Bet knew this, she'd seen it the previous morning, tastefully tied up with pink ribbon, on Liza's dressing-table. So the bitch *was* responsible for Tib's disappearance! Bet had known it all along, really, but hadn't quite liked to suggest it to the others. Liza must have found Tib in her bedroom and chased him out, then . . . What? And, as usual, it was all Bet's fault; she should have foreseen it, she should have kept Tib away from her.

That was Wednesday.

On Friday morning there was still no sign of Tib; everyone but Bet went shopping, Pete having promised them lunch in The George afterwards. Bet said she would rather stay at home; Tib might turn up, or someone ring with news; besides, the men were coming to erect the marquee at two. No one bothered to press her, in fact they all looked rather relieved.

It was while she was weeding the stocks in the bed by the front door, trying ineffectively to make her mind a blank, that Simon drove up. He was alone, and for the first time since Bet had known him, looked his age. 'Bet, I'm so frightfully sorry about Tib, I only heard this morning. Why on earth didn't someone ring the Manor? I've been in London, but Cyn has contacts everywhere – someone's bound to have spotted him.

This was too much! And what was all this rubbish about being in London? How dare he make such a fool of her! She got up off her knees – no position to be in when dealing with the likes of Simon – and ignoring that inner voice urging her to be careful, said, 'Do you really mean to stand there and pretend your girlfriend didn't tell you? But perhaps it's not so surprising, really, as she's the one responsible for Tib's disappearance. I bet she didn't tell you that, did she? She hated him; only the other day Diz caught her throwing stones at him. Then when he stole her miserable chocolates while we were out, she must have frightened him so much he ran away.'

162

'I assume you're referring to Liza Dupont,' Simon blinked and shook his head as though he had bees in his ears. 'Before we go any further with this asinine conversation I should like to make one point quite clear. Liza Dupont is not my girlfriend, she has never been my girlfriend, I do not go in for girlfriends, as you ought to know by now. I came round here on a purely friendly basis to say how sorry I was to hear about Tib and to offer to help find him. I did not come round here to be forced to listen to a lot of baseless accusations from a neurotic, menopausal idiot whose only real gripe against a girl is that she's young, pretty and half her age.'

Now Bet's eyes were opened! Now she saw the wretch in his true colours at last! She was so angry she thought she might quite possibly go mad. 'How . . . how *dare* you speak to me like that! It's because I'm alone, isn't it, with no one to defend me? And because you and your bloody family think they own this place and everyone in it. Well, here's one inhabitant you don't own, and let me tell you, Simon Morris, if I ever see your face round here again I'll — '

'For Christ's sake, Bet, take a grip on yourself and stop carrying on like some half-witted heroine in a soap opera! If that's how you feel about me, it's a pity you didn't say so before, it would have saved us both a lot of bother. I'd no idea you were such a snob; always the same with these pinko-liberals, scratch one, and underneath there's a true blue Tory struggling to get out. Now, if you'll excuse me I've a few more starving tenants to evict before lunch.'

It was at this point that Simon made his mistake. Having refused to take Bet seriously, he turned his back on her. And the second he did so, Bet, the pent up rage of months erupting round her like a fire-cracker out of control — rage against Simon, against Liza, even against Miles for leaving her to battle on alone with powers she didn't understand and wasn't equipped to deal with; but above all, rage against herself for being such a stupid, neurotic fool — was on him with such force that Simon, taken by surprise at the savagery of her attack, was knocked humiliatingly to the ground.

Bet, triumphant, watched him grovel.

Not, however, for long. In a flash, spitting pebbles and grit, he was up and had struck her so hard across the face that she fell back into the flowerbed. 'I'm not a gentleman, Bet, in case you didn't know that already; if a woman hits me, I hit back, only harder. And next time your bloody little dog goes missing, don't expect any help from me.' With that, he climbed rapidly into his car, slammed the door and drove out through the front gate so fast he smashed his wing-mirror on the gatepost.

Bet, her face streaked with mud and tears, her rage turned to ashes, sat in the flowerbed and watched him go. It was only later that she began to wonder where Liza had been that morning, and if she wasn't with Simon, where was she?

Chapter Fifteen

Wind groaning through summer greenery, black clouds chasing each other across a storm-yellow sky; the day of the fête at last.

'What a super morning!' Nell, Mothercare incarnate, bounced into the kitchen where Bet, feeling as if she'd been run through a mincer not once but several times over, crouched over yesterday's *Guardian* and a cup of black coffee. 'You could have fooled me.'

'Oh Mum, do snap out of it, things can't be that bad. Honestly, I sometimes think you enjoy being miserable. Anyway, here's some news to cheer you up; Bern and me are friends again — isn't that great? He says he can't think what got into him, he says he must have been mad.' Bet grunted. 'Do you know, Mum, I really believe it's worth having a row now and again, it's so absolutely wonderful when you make it up.'

God, the egotism of one's children. Did they even consider one might have a life outside their petty little orbit? That if one's silly daughter makes it up with her silly husband it isn't the be-all and end-all of one's existence?

'Morning all.' Bernie now, more bright-eyed and bushy-tailed than Nell, if that were possible, raining kisses on the back of his wife's neck. 'What a super aroma of coffee — I could eat a house.'

Bet fled.

'Now then, everyone, I don't want to make a speech, but I should just like to say I'm counting on you all to do your bit this afternoon. I'm afraid the weather forecast is not too good, but I'm sure you won't let that get you down, and they're always wrong anyway.' The audience laughed dutifully. This was Pol's eve-of-fête pep-talk and she was damned well going to make the most of it.

'I thought she said she wasn't making a speech,' Bet whispered to Don Stewart, who happened to be sitting next to her. 'Splendid stuff though,' he whispered back, 'reminds me of my National Service days, we had a C.O. — '

'Is that correct, Mr Stewart?' Don jumped guiltily. 'You've volunteered to fill the fortune-telling slot? I'm afraid I found your writing a little difficult to read.' Pol held up the questionnaire she'd efficiently issued to all would-be helpers. 'Er, yes, I studied the subject a little in my army days; tarot cards and so forth, you know the sort of thing.'

'Shouldn't a fortune-teller be a lady?' This from Emmie Stokes in the back row, her remark greeted with a faint titter. Pol sighed. 'Unfortunately there've been no lady volunteers for the job. Now, Mr Stewart,' she turned briskly to the cringing Don, 'I'm afraid you'll have to make do with the old outside loo, there's no room for a tent.'

'Won't it be rather a squash. I mean . . .' But Pol had already swept on to more important matters.

'I've had about enough of this,' Bet whispered, 'let's go and make some coffee.' They crept away.

'I gather the French piece is doing a belly-dance?' said Don as they walked across the lawn.

'Oh really, I wouldn't know.'

Damn! He'd put his foot in it again. He longed to take her in his arms, kiss her better, find her dog, murder Simon Morris — anything, just to make her smile again. You've got it bad, old son, he thought, you've got it bad.

'Come on,' she said, 'I'll show you the outside loo, it's lucky you're on the small side.' Don smiled wrily, then remembered that the bastard Morris was none too tall himself. He tentatively took her hand. 'Lead on, then, I'd like to know what I've let myself in for.'

'Morning, Mrs Brandon, any news of your little dog?' It was

Mr Bone, outside the village shop. 'I'm afraid not, we're beginning to give up hope.'

'You mustn't do that, Mrs Brandon, that's not like you,' Mr Bone smiled encouragingly and Bet smiled back. 'How's the baby?'

'Oh fine, absolutely fine. She keeps us awake a bit at nights, but they do, don't they. No, she's great, ever so pretty.' Bet, still smiling, said goodbye and turned away. It wouldn't be too long now before there was a baby at the Rectory; her first grandchild . . . A car swept past her, going much too fast down the village street, Simon at the wheel, unsmiling, ignoring her. A gust of wind caught at her hair and blew raindrops in her face. Arrogant bastard! She turned for home.

Back at the Rectory she was greeted by Nell wearing her will-Mummy-bite-me face. 'Ah, Mum, there you are, I've been looking all over for you.' Oh God, what now? Bet plonked her shopping bag down on the kitchen table. 'I had to go up to the shop, someone seems to have pinched those sausages I'd earmarked for lunch. I do wish people would tell me when – '

'Actually, I think that may have been Bernie.'

'What d'you mean, you think it may have been Bernie – surely you know?'

'Well, yes it was. When he got back from squash last night he felt like a fry-up.'

'I see. Well, I don't want to be difficult, but would he mind awfully in future not – '

'In a way, Mum, that's what I want to talk to you about.'

'What, Bernie's predilection for late-night fry-ups?' She knew she was being unco-operative, but to be reduced to arguing about sausages at this particular moment seemed somehow more than she could bear. 'No, of course not!' Nell, now rather pink in the face, made for the door. 'Anyway, it can wait, I can see you're busy and – '

'Nell, will you please tell me whatever it is you've come to tell me. I'm perfectly able to talk while I'm scrubbing new potatoes, and if you've been hunting all over the place for me, it must be important.'

'Let me help you then.'

'If you must, but there's only one brush and – '

167

'Mum, Bern and I have been discussing things.'

'Oh?'

'About when the baby's born and I'm at home all day. We were — that is, Bern was, and I agree with him — thinking along the lines of perhaps — subject to your consent, of course — converting this part of the house into two self-contained flats. Bern says there'd be plenty of room to have one on each floor. It might be easier if we had the ground floor and you and Diz the first floor, but of course you can choose. He says as the place is now, there's an awful lot of wasted space, so it wouldn't be hard to do, and if you agree, he'd like to start shopping around for estimates as soon as possible. We wouldn't want to hurry you, but — '

'But you'd like it all over and done with before the baby's born?' Was this how one felt after being told one's right arm must come off — nothing? Except perhaps cold fear about what one would feel when one came back to life.

'Well, yes, that's the idea. Then you won't have to go through all the business of coping with a new-born baby again; I mean, I should think you must have had enough of that with Diz and me.'

What you're really saying is, you don't want to have me to cope with as well as a new-born baby ... But of course Bet didn't say that; she might be an idiot, but not that kind of an idiot. Instead she went on scrubbing potatoes, and — trying to keep the tremble out of her voice, and with as much enthusiasm as she could muster — said that to have two separate flats seemed an absolutely splendid idea and the answer to all their problems; indeed, she wondered why no one had thought of it before. There was, as far as she could see, only one possible stumbling block, and that no doubt solvable. How much did Bernie reckon it would all cost?

'Well,' and the relief in Nell's voice was so obvious it was painful, 'he doesn't think that's too much of a problem. If we try and keep the costs down to a minimum, and he does the decorating, he thinks we could probably get away with ...'

But Bet was no longer listening. She was thinking about Tib.

'You look a little faint, dear, why not sit down for a minute and let Mrs Kettle take over?'

'I'm perfectly all right, Mrs Snately, just a bit tired, that's all.' The fête was in full swing now and it was sweltering in the tea tent, the smell of squashed grass and sweat mingling unpleasantly with frying hamburgers. Bet felt hot and sticky all over.

'Sugar down the end,' she shouted above the din, handing three cups of tea to a huge woman in an orange silk dress, 'spoon on a string by the urn.'

'Now, dear, I really must insist you take a rest, I can't have you passing out on me.'

'Honestly, I'm fine, and it wouldn't be fair on Mrs Kettle.'

'Very well then, if you won't take a break, perhaps you could get some more cups, the washers-up are a bit behind. The caterers left some spares in your kitchen, and a breath of fresh air would do you good.'

Dismissed, Bet gave in.

The atmosphere outside the marquee was little better; it would thunder before the day was out. She'd go the long way round through the vegetable garden, there'd be fewer people about.

'Bet, where on earth are you off to? I thought you were supposed to be doing your stint in the tea tent.' Pol, like all good organisers, seemed to be everywhere at once. 'I'm fetching some cups, if you must know. I think Mrs Snately wanted to get rid of me, she kept telling me I looked ill.'

'I suppose you know what's happened?'

'What?' Actually, she couldn't care less if the whole place caught fire and burned down.

'Pete's somehow managed to get himself drunk.'

'So what's new?'

'Bet, do pull yourself together, if only for the sake of our reputation in the village − '

'For heaven's sake, Pol, you sound like someone out of a Trollope novel ...' But Pol wasn't listening. 'He's been judging the home-made wine competition. Of course you're not supposed to drink the wine, just spit it out, but you know Pete.' Bet nodded; she knew Pete. 'Well, he persuaded Bernie to try some, then that wretched Don Stewart turned up, he said he didn't seem to be getting any customers; frankly, I'm not in the least surprised, I'm pretty sure he doesn't know the first thing about telling fortunes, let alone tarot cards. And now all three of them are behaving like a lot of idiotic schoolboys. You'll just have to pull yourself together, Bet, and help me, I simply cannot cope with them on my own.'

Back in Pol's kitchen, Bernie had disappeared, but Pete and Don were leaning against the draining-board gazing owlishly at the row of neatly labelled bottles drawn up in front of them on the kitchen table. 'Rhubarb and damson, gooseberry and prune,' intoned Pete in his comic Church-of-England-vicar voice, a glass of greenish liquid trembling in his hand. 'Date and doughnut, plumbago and pomegranate — '

'Redford, I don't think that last one's quite right.' Don, minus his spectacles, was holding a half-empty bottle up to the light. 'Isn't plumbago some sort of shrub? I'm not sure if you can eat its fruit, I'm not sure if it *has* fruit . . .'

Suddenly, blessedly, a spurt of laughter bubbled up inside Bet. Ratty and Toad! Ratty and Toad from *The Wind in the Willows*! But if Pete were Toad and Don Ratty, who was Mole? Who indeed?

'Bet! My poor, sad little Bet! Come here, ducky, come to your Uncle Pete,' Pete had seen her and lunged forward, arms flailing. 'Leave me alone, you great idiot!' Bet, her laughter quickly turning to outrage, wriggled expertly out of Pete's grasp, at the same time giving him a violent push. The effect of this was rather more than she'd bargained for; he staggered back and then, like some giant ninepin, keeled heavily over on to the floor where he sat, immobilised, his head resting against the back of one of Pol's spindly chairs, staring glassily in front of him.

There was a horrified silence. This sort of thing simply did not happen to Pete. He got drunk, of course — all the time — but never like this; this was unprecedented. What were they to do with him — what could they do with him? They looked at him helplessly, three acolytes gathered round their tribal deity, waiting, awestruck, for him to speak. Nothing happened. In the end it was Pol who brought them down to earth. 'I don't wish to appear ungrateful, Don, but I cannot help thinking that this is your doing.' That's right, dear, thought Bet, when in doubt always blame someone else. 'I left you to keep an eye on my husband for just five minutes, while

I organised refreshments for the Morris Dancers, you promised faithfully you'd make him some black coffee and try to get things going again, and this is what happens.'

'I am most fearfully sorry, Pol. I really did my best, but in mitigation I must say that I do feel something's gone wrong with that particular wine. I've never — '

'If that's the case, all I can say is, why were you and Pete drinking it? But there's no time to go into all that now. As you're here, perhaps you would be good enough to help clear up some of this mess,' she pointed angrily to the contents of a bottle of elderberry wine knocked over in Pete's fall, which was spreading in a sticky crimson tide over the otherwise pristine kitchen floor. 'We'll have to leave my husband where he is for the moment, he's much too heavy to move and I really cannot face another accident.'

'Of course.' Don seized a cloth and started scrubbing, his efforts met by an agonised shriek from Pol. '*Not* my best glass cloth ...!' Bet decided it was time to leave. In any case, wasn't she supposed to be collecting some cups? On her way out she took a quick swig of the rhubarb and dandelion; it was, predictably, disgusting.

Arriving in her own kitchen, she found Liza, still in her Egyptian belly-dancer's outfit, assisted by, of all people, Alfonso — in skin-tight black jeans and a pink shirt — washing up cups. What the hell was Alfonso doing there? Had he been sent by Simon as some kind of peace offering? Was that how the upper classes salved their guilty consciences, by lending out their servants? Come on, Brandon, take a grip on yourself; after all's said and done, you are the one in charge.

'May one ask what you're doing in my kitchen, Liza?'

'Mrs Snately, she want more cups. She said to find you, but you were not 'ere.'

'Well, I'm here now, so perhaps you will take the cups you've done back to Mrs Snately in the tea tent with my compliments, and tell her I'll be along shortly with the rest.'

'But Mrs Snately, she says — '

'I'm not interested in what Mrs Snately says. Will you please take the cups and go.'

Liza, shaking her bangles, gave one of her shrugs and said something to Alfonso in rapid Spanish. He made no

171

comment, merely glanced at Bet, his face as impassive as a Buddha's. Then, after wiping his hands in a finicky sort of way on the grubby roller towel hanging on the back door, he flicked his fingers at Liza in a gesture presumably intended to indicate that she should follow him — which, surprisingly, and pretty meekly for her, she did — picked up the tray of clean cups, and swaying slightly at the hips, slid out of the room.

'Everything all right?' A diffident voice behind her; could she never escape? It was Don. 'I'm afraid your sister's a bit miffed about all this, but it genuinely wasn't my fault. Pete and Bernie were already too far gone by the time I got there. She ordered me to sober them up, but — '

'You decided to join them instead.'

'I didn't have much option. Before I knew where I was, Pete had thrust this glass in my hand; he said it was parsley wine and he wanted another opinion. Well, I've never tasted anything like it in my life. I've worked all over the world, drunk every type of fire-water, but I'll tell you this, Bet, that stuff beat the lot.' He looked at her sadly, swaying a little. 'You know, you have the most beautiful eyes. I suppose you've been told that hundreds of times, but it does happen to be true.' He took a step forward and removed his glasses, they seemed to be getting a bit steamed up.

'Shouldn't you get back to your crystal ball?' Bet poked him gently in the chest. 'There are probably lots of people waiting.'

'I doubt it. I wasn't much good at it, you know.'

'Hullo, Liza, how about a nice pink teddy to take back to Maman in Paris?' Simon, weighed down with prizes he'd won at the shooting range, bumped into a stormy-eyed Liza behind the tea tent. Winning at shooting ranges was one of the things Simon always did — it drove people mad. Liza hunched her shoulders and wriggled her bottom irritably. 'Please do not make fun of me, Simon, I do not want your stupid teddy, I am not a child.'

'So what's got into you, then? Alfonso playing up? If you must go in for these passionate Latins — '

'Alfonso, he is a pig — I hate him!'

172

'Bit of a change of heart, isn't it? Last time I saw you, you were — '

'I do not wish to speak of the Spaniard, Simon, he is a peasant and of no importance.'

'Got up your nose, has he? I'm not surprised, he certainly gets up mine.' Simon tried unsuccessfully to drag his eyes away from the perfect curve of Liza's breasts glimpsed tantalisingly through the folds of her orange T-shirt. Liza, noticing, stroked the teddy. 'But you, Simon, you are not a peasant, you are a *grand seigneur*. Me, I have seen those grandfathers on the walls of your manor house.'

'Ancestors, you stupid chit, and believe me, I'm no *grand seigneur*.'

'Take me away from here, Simon, this fête is boring and stupid. Mrs Brandon, she does not want you now. I see her with that Mr Stewart, they were — '

'Let's leave Mrs Brandon out of it, shall we?' Oh what the hell! What was he doing here anyway? He thought for a minute and then gave in. 'OK then, Mamselle Dupont, let's go somewhere and drown our sorrows in drink! But I warn you, if Alfonso turns up I'm not staying around to have my throat cut. One whiff of his garlic-laden breath and I'm off.'

'Do not worry,' Liza, her scowls miraculously turned to smiles, wound her arms round Simon's neck, 'the Spaniard, he will not come after us, he is busy at his work. Besides, how shall he know where we have gone? You take me somewhere nice, eh?' Simon sighed, unwound the arms and patted her on the rump. 'Well, I don't know about nice,' he said, leading the way to the car park, 'but at least it will be different.'

In the tea tent the afternoon was nearly over, helpers were already busy counting the day's takings and finishing up the leftovers. In a corner Angela Snately was expertly sorting out change. 'Ah, Mrs Brandon, there you are — we'd quite given you up. Never mind, your little French girl has been helping us out. I simply don't know what we would have done without her. She tells me that poor Mr Redford has been taken ill . . .'

'At least we made more than they did last year, and that's without Cyn Westover's cheque. Everyone worked like an

173

absolute Trojan, but then one knew they would.' Did one? 'With the possible exception of one or two members of this family, that is.'

'I take it you're referring to me?' Bet and Pol were having a post mortem in Bet's kitchen, while she listlessly fried hamburgers for Diz and JP who were off to a Saturday night disco in Stotleigh and, despite the fact that they'd been eating all day, wanted a meal before they went.

'Not entirely you.' Pol put down her mug of tea and stood up. 'There were others who weren't much better, and at least you had some excuse. I just don't know how that wretched man had the gall to show his face here.'

'If you mean Simon, I didn't know he had.'

'Oh Bet, I'm so sorry. I thought you must have seen him, I'd never have mentioned it otherwise. The last thing I want to do is upset you.'

'For God's sake, Pol, I'm not sixteen years old! I'm not going to burst into tears every time anyone mentions Simon's name. He's as much right to come to the fête as anyone else; after all, his bloody family more or less own the village.'

'I sometimes wonder if I can do anything right in this house!' Pol was overwrought, puce in the face, and all set for a scene. 'Aren't you even glad I'm on your side? I mean, I would have thought you might be grateful — '

'Grateful — *grateful*!' Bet turned, fish-slice at the ready, dripping hamburger grease all over the kitchen mat. 'Why should I be grateful?'

'Hullo, girls — everything OK?' Pete, miraculously recovered, naked except for a bath towel round his middle and for once without a drink in his hand, stood in the doorway. 'Look, Pol ducky, Lavy Nicholson's just been on the blower. Change of plan for tonight. Would we meet her and Fruity for a noggin in their local instead of up at the house. Then we can all go on together from there. She didn't say why, perhaps old Fruity's run out of booze — seems unlikely, but . . . ' He paused, looking from one sister to the other. 'Now don't tell me you two have been fighting again! If so, I'm off, I still feel too frail to cope with flying crockery.'

But Pol was already at the door, handkerchief in hand and dangerously near to tears. 'We're not quarrelling . . . Anyway, she started it. All I was doing was trying to help; that's all I ever do.'

'Now, now, ducky, you've been marvellous, absolutely marvellous; we all think so, don't we, Bet?' Bet slapped the hamburgers on a plate and cracked a couple of eggs into the pan. 'Yes, we think you're marvellous, Pol, didn't you know,' she said in the flattest of flat voices while she peered at the spluttering eggs. Pol went on standing by the door, bosom heaving, dabbing her eyes with her handkerchief, then with a shriek of, 'Hypocrites!' she fled, slamming the door behind her.'

'Bet, ducky . . .' Pete loomed reproachfully.

'If you're going to tell me I'm a bitch, don't bother, I know already.' Green eyes turned on Pete, misty with tears and pain.

'Oh *ducky* . . .'

Chapter Sixteen

Hours later − or at least, that was what if felt like − Bet heard the phone ringing in the empty house. Everyone else was out somewhere, having a good time, and Bet, supperless, was sitting alone in the kitchen with a glass of gin and tonic for company. She'd bought the gin that morning with the sausages, feeling she might need it to cope with today, and she'd been right. The tonic was a bit flat, but it was the gin that counted, wasn't it? The phone went on ringing. Hell! She'd have to answer it; if she didn't, she'd only wish she had as soon as it stopped ringing.

'Bet? Don. Don Stewart here. Hope I'm not interrupting a meal or anything?'

'Oh hullo, Don. No, you're not interrupting anything.' Better not say she was alone, he might want to come round and she didn't think she could face that. 'Have you recovered?'

'Yes thanks. I dosed myself liberally with black coffee as soon as I got home and I feel as right as rain now.'

'Oh good.' Silence at the other end. 'Look, Don, I don't want to sound rude, but I am rather tired. What exactly did you −?'

'Actually, I wanted to apologise for this afternoon.'

'For getting sloshed on home-made plonk? Hardly your fault, by all accounts.'

'More for trying to make a pass at you.'

'But you didn't, you behaved with the utmost decorum.'

'I told you you had beautiful eyes. Well, you do, but it was neither the time nor the place to tell you so.'

'Don't give it another thought; it's always nice to receive compliments.'

'As a matter of fact, there is one more thing.'

'Yes?'

'It's just . . . well, I know you're in love with someone else so probably not in the least interested — will no doubt think me the most frightful bore for bringing it up in the first place. But the fact is, I seem to have fallen in love with you and . . . I'd like you to know that if you ever need a shoulder to cry on, I'll be there — that's all.'

But she wasn't in love with someone, not any more, she knew that now. They'd been right, damn them; her great affair with Simon Morris had been nothing more than a stupid infatuation after all, and would never have stood the test of time, and Dr Ram's warning about the psyche playing strange tricks had been spot on. But why didn't this knowledge make her feel better; why did she feel so awful; why did she feel such a fool? She ran her fingers through her hair and looked down at the hole in the loose floorboard underneath the telephone table; she must remember to have it seen to. Except that of course she needn't bother now, need she. Soon this would be part of the Sparsworth domain, she and Diz banished upstairs. And next year, with Diz away at university, there would be only her; a solitary granny in her granny flat . . .

'Bet, are you still there?'

'Yes, of course I am. I was just trying to think what to say. And if by "a shoulder to cry on", you mean what I think you mean, then the answer is — '

'Of course I didn't mean that! I can't have made myself clear, please understand — '

'I'm sorry, Don. I know you mean well, but I'm tired, I've got a headache and I can't think straight about anything at the moment, so can we leave it at that? Now, if you don't mind, I really must go,' and she gently replaced the receiver.

'Bloody hell!' shouted Don to his terrier, Rex, who looked surprised. Then he just went on sitting there in front of his elderly portable typewriter, gazing gloomily at the now silent telephone. He hadn't intended to ring her in the first place, and he certainly hadn't intended to say what he had said.

177

What had got into him? Did he have to keep on making such a fool of himself? He brooded on this for a moment, then decided that unfortunately – or fortunately, if you looked at the thing from the other way round – the answer seemed to be yes. So be it.

Bet was alone again, and the silence of the house was now so thick you could cut it with a knife. She supposed she should eat; life, after all, had to go on. But did it? Did life have to go on? Who said so, and why? Back in the kitchen, she poured herself another drink and decided she didn't know the answer and was too tired to try and work one out. Then, collecting a plate of tea-tent left-overs – two rock-hard rock cakes and a squashed sausage roll – she put them and her drink on a tray and wandered into her sitting-room. Late evening sun shone through the two long windows, illuminating the soft, rich colours of the Persian rugs and highlighting the dust on the furniture. The room smelt of damp and roses; it seemed a long time since she'd last sat down in it.

It was while she was moving the several volumes of Parson Woodforde's Diaries – still unread – from the table by Miles's chair to make room for the tray, that she came upon the postcard of Cosimo Medici. She remembered now, she'd found it months ago in a pile of old letters in the attic, and must have stuck it in Parson Woodforde as a bookmark. Holding it up to the light, she tried to discern the likeness, once seen, to Simon. But the clever, patrician face with its dark curling beard and scarlet cap, stared back at her mockingly; there was certainly no resemblance now – how could she ever have thought they looked alike? Sadly she returned the postcard to its place in Parson Woodforde. Perhaps now she would get round to reading him at last; there would be plenty of time in the long months to come. Then, worn out with absolutely everything, tearless and supperless and more than a little drunk, she sat down in Miles's chair, closed her eyes and instantly fell asleep.

Suddenly, she was jerked into unwilling consciousness by the raucous sound of the backdoor buzzer. Who the hell could that be at this hour? Perhaps if she ignored it, whoever it was would give up and go away. She tried, leaning back in the chair and closing her eyes again; it buzzed once more, louder than ever. No use, she'd have to rouse herself and go and see who it was. Feeling ghastly, she hauled herself to her feet, peered briefly at her wan, smudged face in the mirror over the mantlepiece, gave up on it, and tottered into the kitchen.

Opening the backdoor she discovered Mr Bone, resplendent in lime-green vest and pinstripes, about to press the buzzer again.

'Oh, hullo,' Bet blinked muzzily at him. This was all she needed.

'Sorry to bother you so late, Mrs Brandon; it's about your little dog.'

'You've found the body?'

'No, no, nothing like that,' Mr Bone made soothing noises, 'only I was talking to old Zach Keeble in The Waggoner just now. Old Zach doesn't get out much these days, but it's the old chap's birthday so some of the lads were buying him a drink.' Bet nodded impatiently. 'Well, we got talking about your Tib and how you'd lost him, like, and Zach said Had you tried the old lime-burner's cottage in the woods? He said what made him think of it was that some visitors lost their dog a while back, when they were down here on holiday; had to go home without him. Then months after, a couple of lads broke into the old cottage and found the dog's remains. They reckoned it must have got in there somehow, and then couldn't get out.'

'And you're saying the same thing's happened to Tib?' Mr Bone nodded, trying not to be aware of the look of horror on Bet's face. He pressed on. 'Early days yet, Mrs Brandon, if the dog is there, he's most likely still alive. That's why I came straight round — your boys could go up now, have a look before it gets too dark.'

'They're out, and won't be back for hours yet. I'll have to go myself.'

'Not on your own, Mrs Brandon, you can't go on your own. I'd come with you, but the wife and me are on our way to visit friends, we're late already and —' Bet nodded abstractedly. 'Of course you mustn't think of it, I'll be perfectly all right, I know the wood quite well. It's just that I never knew there was a cottage —'

'In the old lime pit, Zach says, up the north-east corner on the Manor side. He says the pit's so filled up with trees and bushes now, you'd never know there was a cottage ... All the same, better wait till morning.'

'Look, Mr Bone, if Tib is there, he'll certainly be nearly dead from starvation, if not already dead. A few hours might make all the difference.' A horn tooted in the lane. Mr Bone looked harassed and said he was sorry but he had to go ... The wife, you see ...

Bet, intoxicated, this time with excitement, had already forgotten his existence. She knew with complete certainty that she would find Tib in the old cottage. Whether he would be alive or dead was another matter, but he'd be there. She dashed upstairs, threw on an old pair of trousers, a thick sweater and her red anorak, rushed downstairs, scribbled a note for the children, found, after some rummaging, a torch that worked, and put on her wellingtons. Then she rushed upstairs again to fetch Tib's blanket from his basket; he might just be still alive and she would need something to wrap him in.

Her preparations complete at last, she locked the back door, put the key under the geranium tub and set out for the woods.

'Simon, there is something in my sandal ... There is blood. Let us go back, I do not like this place.'

'Oh don't whinge! Come on, only another few minutes, we must be nearly there. I thought you said you wanted some excitement.'

'You said to find old the cottage in the woods and have a picnic — this would be romantic. It is not romantic, Simon, it is stupid. You did not say there would be thorns and nettles, you said ...'

Simon gave up listening. They'd reached the bottom of the steps cut into the quarry face, and ahead of them the path into the old lime pit was barely discernible under the mat of brambles, thorn bushes and outsize stinging-nettles. Surely it never used to be as bad as this, not in the old days? Perhaps Liza was right, perhaps they shouldn't have come. Then, just as he was about to call a halt, the path twisted suddenly to avoid the remains of a battered holly bush, and there in front of them was the cottage.

'Do you know, I don't think I've been here since I was eleven years old.' Liza shrugged and went on examining her cuts. 'Nothing like a spot of enthusiasm, I always say. What's happened to all that Gallic charm?' Simon peered through the windows, then gave the front door a kick; it creaked slowly open. Somewhere in the ivy above it, something rustled.

Inside smelt of damp and rotting vegetation. Mildewed wallpaper hung in brown strips from the bulging walls of the dark little room, and remnants of lace curtain smothered in cobwebs and defunct flies adhered to one of the tiny windows. A door let out of the back, and a rickety stair-case led to the two bedrooms upstairs. It was very cold.

'Come on then, let's open that wine and try to make things a bit more comfortable.' Simon slung the haversack of wine on the floor and rubbed his hands with an enthusiasm he didn't really feel. 'You know, we used to have the most marvellous feasts here in the old days, a whole gang of us from the village. It was in Cyn's commando phase; we turned the lime pit into an assault course, and she timed us with Grandpa's stopwatch . . .'

'Simon, this corkscrew, it does not work — see how it grinds the cork in little pieces.'

But Simon wasn't listening, he was looking round the poky little room, trying in vain to recapture the sense of wonder and excitement he'd felt there as a boy so long ago. He remembered Cyn, a stocky figure in baggy flannel shorts, a red Alice-band holding back her golden hair, putting away the stopwatch and taking off her Aertex shirt to reveal her beautiful twelve-year-old's breasts. A glimpse of these — you could only touch them if you won three times — was the ultimate prize in the game — the fastest man round the course allowed to view them for one minute only. He'd cheated once and quickly been demoted. 'Si, that's not fair, you must always play the game properly or not at all,' Cyn had said when she found out, and he'd been near to tears. What was he doing here now, what in hell's name was he doing? He looked at Liza and suddenly realised he didn't even like her. In fact, not to put too fine a point on it, he found her a crashing bore.

Yet here he was, performing the same old routine just one more time. Tomorrow he'd go away again; back to hotel rooms, bars, other people's flats. He'd never write his book, he'd always be the clown who wanted to play Hamlet but somehow couldn't bring himself even to try; the little wop, the organ grinder's monkey . . .

'Come on then, you lazy bitch, hurry up with that wine.' Behind him Liza put her arms round his neck. 'Love me, Simon, love me now . . .'

Simon closed his eyes. 'Oh, all right then . . . If we must. And then we'll have the wine . . .'

Bet, mud on her boots from the tramp across the field, reached the wood in record time. Despite a hangover of fairly horrific proportions, and an empty stomach, she felt exhilarated. Because she was doing something positive at last, she supposed. Had she ever done anything positive before? Cleaning the mud off her boots on a handy tussock, she racked her brains. What about joining the CND? That time she'd gone on the Aldermaston March. Miles hadn't wanted her to go; civil servants, he'd said, shouldn't get involved in politics. She wasn't a civil servant, she'd said, she was a civil servant's wife, and CND wasn't politics, it was the future of mankind; and she'd gone. Miles hadn't spoken to her for a week, and she'd sprained her ankle somewhere just outside Reading and had to be brought back home in an ambulance.

She dived into the wood.

What seemed hours later, with her heart hammering and blood on her cheek from a passing bramble, limping slightly and sticky with sweat, she finally caught up with the old lime pit. It was dusk now, and behind her the wood breathed a life of its own; wind scratched at the ash poles, leaves rustled, twigs snapped. There were other noises, too; slightly more nerve-racking noises whose origins one couldn't begin to guess at — even if one wanted to, and one didn't.

In front of her was the lime pit. Enclosed by a barbed wire fence, it was much bigger than she'd envisaged. Quite tall trees grew up from the bottom, and the sides, although in places not particularly steep, were so smothered in rampaging undergrowth, mostly of the prickly variety, as to appear at first sight impassable. Although less overgrown, the far side, bordering on the Manor fields, was a more or less vertical quarry face, and out of the question unless one happened to be an experienced climber. How could Tib possibly have got into such a place? And — supposing he had — how could she follow him?

Come on, Brandon, you can't give up now; if someone managed to build a cottage down there, there must be a way in. OK, that was years ago, but what about the boys who broke in and found that other dog? Oh God — that other dog ...

Spurred on by the thought of Tib's sad predecessor, Bet hurried along the perimeter of the pit, searching for a way in. The trouble was that in the dark things tended to merge into each other, and if she didn't find a place more or less at once, she would have to wait until morning. Then, quite suddenly, there were these two trees, and between them, incredibly, invitingly, a path. One had to admit one couldn't quite see where the path went, but where else could it go but down? This must be the way Tib came — it simply had to be.

With Tib's blanket round her waist, Bet, triumphant, squeezed under the wire. There, all it needed was a little effort; plain sailing now. The path even looked as though it was used quite frequently. It got steep, of course, very steep actually, but it would, wouldn't it. Then, about twenty yards down, without warning, without so much as a by-your-leave, the damn thing fizzled out. One minute it was there, the next it had vanished under a ten-foot wall of blackberry bushes. Like so much else in Bet's present existence, it had turned out to be a red herring after all.

So this was it then, she was beaten. She sat back on her heels and started to cry, and once started, couldn't stop. Nothing more she could do now but go home with her tail between her legs — if indeed she could find her way home, which was doubtful. She should have waited for the children, rung Don, used her common sense. Instead of which, she'd behaved like the irresponsible idiot she was; proving once and for all something she'd been aware of for some time now, namely, that Bet Brandon, independent, intelligent, caring housewife and mother, was nothing but a fraud. Take away her props, first Dad, then Miles, and where was she? Where indeed? She was like a canary let out of its cage, not knowing what to do but blunder about and bump into the furniture. Look at me, I can fly – or at least, I'll be able to just as soon as someone tells me how, and someone else holds my hand while I'm doing it ...

Now she was Bet the loser; eyes shut, cheeks wet, crouching by her wall of blackberries; the lowest of the very low, down for a count of ten, waiting for the bell to ring and tell her it was all over, she didn't have to bother any more ...

She went on crouching.

Was it the cold, or cramp in her foot that, aeons later, made her open her eyes; or was it the newly risen moon shining on her face? Whatever it was, she opened them, and suddenly, without warning, like a trout leaping high out of the river in its search for evening flies, or a rocket whooshing into the sky trailing behind it a sheaf of coloured stars, a thought popped up from the muddy depths of Bet's soul. She was alive! She wanted to be alive, and what was more, she was damned well going to stay alive.

Bet grinned to herself in the darkness. Then, rubbing her poor cramped foot, she decided on one last look for a gap in the wall of bushes in front of her. If there wasn't one, so be it, she'd call it a day. In any case, the kids would surely have seen her note by now – might have started out to look for her.

But of course there was a gap; there had to be, didn't there? And there it was, only a few feet from where she'd been crouching. A tiny, prickly gap, just negotiable for a smallish person crawling on her stomach and keeping her eyes shut. The far side of the gap, bright in the moonlight, turned out to be a sloping ledge covered in tussocky grass, trails of old man's beard and rabbit droppings. Scratched and torn from grasping brambles, Bet, triumphant once again, struggled to her feet and, not forty feet below her, saw the ivy-covered chimney of a cottage.

Then it happened. She stepped forward, caught her foot in a rabbit hole, and started to slide. She reached out for something to catch on to, but there was nothing; only falling stones and the wind in her ears. This was it then, was it? Nothing she could do about it, but what a shame it had to happen just as she had come to her senses.

She went on falling.

'I am cold, Simon, my back aches.'

'Do you ever stop moaning?'

'You are cruel and stupid. Alfonso, he is not like this.'

'Bugger Alfonso!' Simon and Liza, chilled to the marrow, were lying on a rug on the cold cottage floor, an empty bottle of wine between them. 'Come on, we'd better make tracks, we must have slept for hours.'

Simon got up stiffly and peered through the filthy windowpane. He longed to be home, seated comfortably by the morning-room fire, a soothing drink in his hand. He must be clean off his trolley, he really must. His body ached all over and it would be worse tomorrow. He'd had these aches and pains lately, he wouldn't be surprised if it wasn't rheumatism — if it wasn't something worse.

'Simon, there is something moving in the room through there.' Liza stood behind him, pointing, her leopard eyes wide with fear.

'Oh, for heaven's sake.'

'I do not like this place, I do not want to go back through all those prickles, I — '

'Shut up a minute.'

Simon could hear it now, a faint whimper and a sort of scrabbling noise — there must be something there after all. Where on earth was the bloody torch? He found it at last at the bottom of the haversack.

'Do not go in there, Simon, someone may be hiding . . .'

The door to the back kitchen refused to move, damp had swollen the timbers and the bolt was rusted in. Simon took a run at it and it gave way suddenly, precipitating him down a couple of broken stone steps on to the earth floor below. He got up painfully, rubbing his knee, and shone the torch round the room. In the corner by the old sink, something that looked like a piece of dirty rag moved slightly and whimpered.

'My God, it's Tib! It's poor little old Tib! Quick, hold the torch while I have a look.' And it was Tib, but only just; a Tib with no more than a thread of life left in him and an ugly gash on his right hind leg. 'Poor, poor old man, poor little old man.' Making soothing noises, Simon very gently picked the little dog up and carried him back into the other room, where he laid him down on the rug. 'I reckon he must have injured that leg in a rock fall and somehow managed to drag himself into the cottage under the back door, then collapsed.' He touched the ugly, gaping wound with his finger and Tib flinched. 'We'll have to try and do some rudimentary repairs to this before we start back. Look, take the torch and a mug, and see if the old rainwater tank is still out at the back.'

'But I cannot go alone, Simon, there will be things out there in the dark.'

'For heaven's sake! What a bloody useless woman you are, to be sure! I'll go, then, and you keep an eye on Tib. There's a candle somewhere in the haversack, we'll need all the light we can get.'

Alone, Liza looked down at Tib with distaste. What a fuss about a smelly little dog! The English, they were so absurd. Now the Spanish ...

There was a small area of ragged grass a few feet square at the rear of the cottage, beyond it the almost vertical quarry face. As Simon emerged from the back door, torch in hand, the moon came out from under a cloud, lighting up the whole area with brilliant clarity. The body of a woman lay spread-eagled on the ground at the foot of the cliff; she wore a red anorak and her hair was powdered with lime dust.

It was Bet.

Chapter Seventeen

'Well, I'll be damned!' Old Monty Cornwall choked over his toast. 'Now what's the matter?' Kitty, deep in her *Daily Mail*, disliked talking at breakfast.

'Cyn Westover's engaged.'

'She can't be.'

'She is — what's more, you'll never guess who to ...' But Kitty was already up and reading over his shoulder.

A marriage has been arranged and will shortly take place between Cynthia Penelope Westover, only daughter of the late Colonel and Mrs Bertram Westover of Hopton Manor, Stotleigh, Suffolk, and Simon Angelo Bertram Morris, only son of Mrs Ann Morris (née Westover) of The Riding School, Shrimpton, Surrey.

'Now there's a turn up for the books.' Kitty sat down rather suddenly and reached for the coffee pot. 'Do you think we'll be invited to the wedding?'

'Put me through to my husband, will you.' His secretary buzzed Pete. 'Fiona, I thought I told you I wasn't taking any calls.'

'It's your wife, Pete, she says it's urgent.'

'Oh, very well then. Hullo, ducky, anything wrong?'

'Have you seen the *Telegraph*?'

'No, I've been absolutely flat out since I got in, in fact I can only talk for a minute —'

'Cyn Westover's engaged.'

'Is she now. Well, I suppose it comes to all of us. She must be fifty if she's a day.'

'She's engaged to Simon Morris.'

'You're having me on.'

'She is — it's here in front of me.'

'Are you sure you've got it right, ducky? I mean — '

'Of course I've got it right. How many Simon Angelo Bertram Morrises d'you think there are?'

'Good Lord, is that the chap's name?'

'What does it matter what his name is, it's Bet I'm worried about. I'm afraid this is going to be a terrible shock; just as she's getting so much better, too. I had a card this morning from the convalescent home, she says it's lovely, and one of the doctors is an absolute dream.'

Pete knew, he'd sent Bet a bunch of roses to await her arrival and she'd rung him at the office to thank him. He hadn't, however, told Pol; she seemed a bit touchy lately, and he'd thought it better not to. 'I don't think we need worry too much on that score, ducky, I fancy Bet went right off the chap in the end. I know he saved her life and all that, but it's quite on the cards she would never have fallen down that damn pit in the first place if she hadn't met him.' He paused for thought. 'I suppose she might have, though. It was the French piece who drove the dog away.'

'Stop waffling, Pete, I thought you said you were busy. What I want to know is, who's going to tell Bet ...'

'But Aunt Pol, are you are sure? I mean, it seems so odd. If they were going to get married, why on earth not years ago. Why wait until they're old ...?'

On the terrace of Napton Park Convalescent Home, Bet lay back in her chair — strategically placed to catch the dying sun — and stretched luxuriously. Before her was a silvan landscape of park and lake laid out exactly as Capability Brown intended. Soon it would be supper, and then bed. She watched the gaunt, grey shape of a heron rise slowly from his post by the reeds at the edge of the lake and flap away towards the distant woods. How beautiful it all was. She sipped her sherry — dry amontillado — and reached for Don Stewart's letter on the table beside her.

188

My dear Bet

Just a line to tell you Tib's progressing like a house on fire. The vet says he'll have to keep the pin in his leg for life, but in a few months time he shouldn't even be lame, and neither he nor anyone else will know it's there. Meanwhile he's managing splendidly on three legs, and much to my surprise, as he's a cantankerous old devil, appears to dote on my terrier, Rex.

I hear from Nell that you too are going on splendidly, which is marvellous news. I shan't forget the night of your accident in a hurry. I don't know if anyone has told you, but I was the person Liza flagged down in the road on her way to get help. I was driving back from Stotleigh after delivering some stuff for typing to Jenny — my more than competent typist — that should have been done the previous week; my masters were beginning to get restive, and Jenny very kindly said she'd make an all-out effort to finish it on the Sunday and then it could go off by first post Monday morning. Of course I stayed longer than I'd meant to — Jenny and Brian are old friends and they offered coffee. Thank God I did! Liza was in a wretched state when I came upon her, wandering along the middle of the road, shoeless, weeping like a water-spout. My French is by no means as fluent as it should be, and she was well past conversing in English, but at least I managed to get the gist of what had happened, and she did have a scrawled note from Simon. Apparently he'd told her to take the footpath out of the wood that leads directly to the Manor and get help pronto, but she'd missed the path in the dark, lost her sandals, been chased by a cow, and eventually landed up on the main road where I found her.

I don't think I've ever driven so fast in my life! My cottage was nearer than the Manor, so we went there. I must say, the emergency services were absolutely first-

189

class, and everyone else was pretty good too. When I got through to Nell, she said the Redfords weren't back from their do yet, but Bernie and the two boys had formed a search-party and were already on their way to the wood. As it turned out, they arrived at the lime pit before the ambulance people and were a tremendous help. As to Cyn Westover, after that dreadful night I'll always regard her as someone I'd like to have beside me in a crisis. The rescue people said that without her detailed knowledge of the terrain, they might well have had to wait until morning to get you and Tib out. By the way, did you know there were hourly bulletins about you both on Radio Stourwick? Fame indeed! Anyway − enough of all that, you've no doubt heard most if it before, in any case.

Things at the Rectory seem to be running with commendable smoothness. I've taken over nursing Tib − although he's way beyond that stage now, and as fit as a flea − because what with one thing and another, Nell has quite a lot on her plate. I also pop over now and again to help out with the garden. I don't think anyone realised just how much work you put into it until you became *hors de combat*.

I've had a card from Diz and JP in the Lakes. They say they're enjoying themselves, but wonder whether it will ever stop raining. What else?

My book moves slowly. I always hate this part. To add to everything else, my publishers are threatening some sort of pre-publication publicity; I always thought they'd get me sooner or later, ours is a strictly love/hate relationship. Anyway, if in two or three months time you happen to come across me sitting all by myself in a bookshop in Stourwick surrounded by unsold copies of my book − take pity!

Sorry to write at such length, but once started, couldn't stop. Sorry too I was unable to visit you in hospital, but the powers-that-be decreed otherwise. However, no such embargo on Napton Park. How about three-fifteen next Wednesday − and would flowers do, or would you prefer books??

All my love − please get well very, very soon −

Don

P.S. Tib sends his love too.

Bet carefully folded the letter and returned it to its envelope. What a nice person he was, and what was more, it seemed as though he really was in love with her. Would she marry him? Well, she might; Miles would approve, she was sure of that. But perhaps she would wait just a little while before she made up her mind. At least until she'd learned to cope with her new-found freedom – new indeed, but nonetheless precious; until she'd had a go at some of those things she was sure now were waiting just round the corner for her to have a go at. That she didn't yet know what the things might be, somehow didn't matter. She knew they would be exciting and demanding and possibly even fun, and that she would do them. Meanwhile ... well, it was great to have found a friend like Don, and she didn't deserve him, or such luck. But then, if everyone came by their deserts ...

Funny, though; he'd been around all through the drama; no one had told her that. But then no one had told her anything much about the night of her accident, and to be honest, she hadn't bothered to ask.

And now for that other letter. The one postmarked Tangier, the one that had come by the second post, and that she hadn't had the courage to open – until now ...

> Villa Backhouse
> PO Box 20
> Tangier
>
> Sunday

My dear Titania

I never write letters and I never apologise, and here I am breaking the habit of a lifetime – you really do have an odd effect on people, don't you. Cyn tells me you're on the mend now, and I'm glad. I shan't forget my last sight of you in a hurry, that's for sure. Nor shall I forget the sight of your family, every man jack of them in varying stages of hysteria, including that love-sick archaeologist of yours. Marry him, Bet, and put the guy out of his misery – for all our sakes.

Now for the apologies, and I can assure you they don't

come easy. I'm sorry, Titania (I can go on calling you Titania, can't I, I seem to have got used to it), sorry for the whole damned stupid mess. I could say we met too late, only it sounds so bloody hackneyed. Things moved so fast, I found I was up to my neck before I knew what was happening, and yet I knew all the time (as I have a feeling you did, too) that it was hopeless, that we'd never make a go of it together. It just wasn't on. Then up comes Mademoiselle Liza Dupont, the perfect let-out. By the way, that girl is absolutely *useless* in a crisis. I'll never forget sitting in that bloody cottage with you and Tib, both in what seemed at the time to be the last stages, wondering whether that stupid little bitch had made it to the Manor, or fallen down a pothole and simply given up. What was I saying? Oh yes. Well, that's how it was and that's how I am, and I assure you I'm not proud of it.

One more thing. I'd better tell you now, you're sure to hear pretty soon anyway, as I don't doubt your sister is a dedicated reader of the *Telegraph*. When I've done here – care-taking for Johnny Backhouse; free food and drink, plus pool, but too many ex-pats around for my liking – Cyn and I are getting married. Don't be too surprised. In a way I suppose it's always been on the cards. Cyn was my first woman and she'll no doubt be my last. We've always got on, in our own weird way, and she doesn't seem too averse to the idea. I have plans, believe it or not, for having a bash at giving poor old Hopton a bit of a face-lift, it needs one badly after years of Cyn in charge; my Dad and I owe it that, at least.

Take care then, Titania. I'll be lord of the manor yet, *and* write a best-seller – you see!

Cheers,

Simon

P.S. By the way, did anyone tell you Liza has run off with Alfonso – or is it vice versa? Whichever way round, I reckon they deserve each other.

P.P.S. Now we're not lovers, let's be friends, eh??? – S.

Bet sat quite still for a moment, the letter on her knee, looking blindly out across the lake. Then slowly, imperceptibly, like the rainbow that follows the storm, she began to smile and then to laugh outright. Indeed, her laughter became so noisy and un-bridled that it disturbed the friendly sparrow perched on the stone balustrade beside her — who, after squirting out a quick message of disapproval, fluffed out his feathers and flew off in a huff. So that was it! Cyn Westover. It was the one thing she'd never thought of, and it had been staring her in the face all the time.

Inside the house a bell rang; she must go in to supper. 'You look happy, Mrs Brandon.' It was lovely Dr Roberts, finishing his rounds. Bet, still giggling, got up stiffly from her chair and reached for her stick. 'It's nothing. Just something rather funny has happened, that's all ...'

'Oh, do stop boring away over those papers, Si, Mr Partridge really does know what he's doing.'

'If Partridge knows what he's doing, then I'm head of the civil service. I've never seen such a bloody cock-up in my life! Now what I'm suggesting is, we dump all this stuff in a cardboard box, put it in the car, and drive the whole lot over to that accountant of Pogo Nicholson's. Pogo says he's damned good, and that if he can't make sense of it, no one can. Then, depending on what he says, we can — '

'Will you shut up, Si, I'm beginning to wish we'd never got married! You're becoming an absolute bore about all this.'

'Nonsense, girl, you love it, you know you do. I can't think why we didn't do it before. I might at least have made a push to prevent the place from collapsing round our ears.'

'Simon Morris, if you don't belt up I'll ... I'll jump on you, and I can promise you you won't like it. I'm a big girl now — '

'You don't need to tell me that, my sweet!'

'I'll kill you, Si, you see ... Oh Si ...'

And the dog, Oxford, waiting patiently to be let out, gave up, finished cleaning the mud from his rear end, put his nose on his paws and went to sleep.

You have been reading a novel published by Piatkus Books. We hope you have enjoyed it and that you would like to read more of our titles. Please ask for them in your local library or bookshop.

If you would like to be put on our mailing list to receive details of new publications, please send a large stamped addressed envelope (UK only) to:

Piatkus Books, 5 Windmill Street
London W1P 1HF

PIATKUS

The sign of a good book